WE WHO
WALK
THE SEVEN
WAYS

WE WHO WALK THE SEVEN WAYS

A Memoir

TERRA TREVOR

University of Nebraska Press · Lincoln

The University of Nebraska Press is part of a land-grant institution with campuses and programs on the past, present, and future homelands of the Pawnee, Ponca, Otoe-Missouria, Omaha, Dakota, Lakota, Kaw, Cheyenne, and Arapaho Peoples, as well as those of the relocated Ho-Chunk, Sac and Fox, and Iowa Peoples.

Library of Congress Cataloging-in-Publication Data
Names: Trevor, Terra, author.
Title: We who walk the seven ways: a memoir / Terra Trevor.
Other titles: We who walk the 7 ways
Description: Lincoln: University of Nebraska Press, [2023]
Identifiers: LCCN 2022034825
ISBN 9781496235183 (paperback)
ISBN 9781496235992 (epub)
ISBN 9781496236005 (pdf)
Subjects: LCSH: Trevor, Terra. | Indian women—California—Biography. | Racially mixed women—California—Biography. | Racially mixed people—California—Biography. | Indian women authors—California—Biography. | Indian authors—California—Biography. | Racially mixed women—Race identity—California. | Racially mixed people—Race identity—California. | Indian women elders (Indigenous leaders)—California. | Chumash Indians—California—Rites and ceremonies. | BISAC: BIOGRAPHY & AUTOBIOGRAPHY / Personal Memoirs | BIOGRAPHY & AUTOBIOGRAPHY / Women
Classification: LCC E78.C15 T74 2023 | DDC 305.48/897092
[B]—dc23/eng/20221220
LC record available at https://lccn.loc.gov/2022034825
Set in Quadraat by A. Shahan.

For my aunties,
who believed I could and taught me how

CONTENTS

AUTHOR'S NOTE

The U.S. Congress passed the Religious Crimes Code in 1883. American Indian people were forbidden to hold religious ceremonies, conduct prayer, or teach children our cultures.

Anyone who did could be put in jail.

The Religious Crimes Code was in effect throughout my childhood, teens, and early adult years.

Joy Harjo writes in *An American Sunrise: Poems*: "Until the passage of the Indian Religious Freedom Act of 1978, it was illegal for Native citizens to practice our cultures. This included the making and sharing of songs and stories. Songs and stories in one culture are poetry and prose in another. They are intrinsic to cultural sovereignty. To write or create as a Native person was essentially illegal."

WE WHO
WALK
THE SEVEN
WAYS

1

WE WHO WALK THE SEVEN WAYS

The Indian in me is strongest. Auntie said there's no such thing as being part Indian. But even before she told me, I already knew, have known forever, the Indian in me is strongest.

Bill said it was important for me to know who I am and not to let my skin color define me. Not to let it define the way other people perceive me when they don't know my story. Although it seemed natural for Auntie to be the one guiding me to walk the sacred hoop, the female cycles of life for Native women, instead, it was my friend Bill, because he led me to the women who showed me the path and picked up where Auntie left off.

Bill was mixed-blood American Indian and Black. I'm an olive-skinned mixed-blood—Cherokee, Lenape, Seneca, and white. He was a journalist, had published five books and taught creative writing. Seventy-two years of the woods and rivers ran in his knowledge. When we first met, I was a young mother-writer. We had weekly chats about writing, but our talks always moved over to conversations about race. I'm always on the verge of figuring out how to live in this world with my complicated racial mix and never quite reaching a satisfying answer.

Then on a Thursday in September, just as the moon was finishing its travels of the night and was ready to lie down in the west, I received the phone call telling me Bill was dead.

2 · WE WHO WALK THE SEVEN WAYS

When Bill died, I was in my late thirties. Now I'm nearing seventy, looking back over three decades at the friendships he guided me into with the elder Native women who informed, instructed, and shaped me into the woman I am today.

After Bill died, I began memorizing everything. Moonlight falling on the tangle of blue morning glory in my backyard. The certain set to my oldest daughter's jaw. Seventeen, her black hair gathered in a ponytail at the nape of her neck, loose strands falling in her face, watching her tucking them behind one ear. We didn't have a reason to suspect it at the time, but it would be the last year she lived with us.

My youngest daughter, thirteen, brown skin tanned, rolling her serious eyes while smearing on strawberry lip gloss. My husband getting up at the first dim light, moving quietly in the dark house making coffee for me.

And the way my eleven-year-old son's black hair shone red in the sun and the freckle on his right cheek. He was recovering after having been diagnosed with a malignant brain tumor. The tumor was resected with surgery, followed by radiation and sixteen months of chemo.

He was no longer bone thin and had gained thirty pounds. The knees of his jeans were streaked with grass stains. Gone were the pristine sick days when his white hooded sweatshirt stayed spotless for weeks at a time. Now, each time he left a muddy footprint on the kitchen floor, I rejoiced.

After my son regained his health, he didn't want to spend his Saturdays with me; he wanted to have playdates with friends, sleepovers, and go to summer camp. My daughters were active teenagers. Regular life was returned to us, and I was getting to know myself on new terms.

It's a medical fact that a mother who is raising a seriously ill child can age faster than her peer group of mothers raising healthy children. Perhaps this is why in 1991, at age thirty-eight, I found my way into the elders' writing circle Bill led on Friday mornings and began making close friendships with women who were in their seventies and eighties.

The shiplap side structure, where Bill taught creative writing, sat atop a hill on land that once belonged wholly to the Indigenous Chumash people. It was surrounded by orange California poppies in the spring and overlooked the Pacific Ocean, with the Channel Islands beyond.

I met Bill before my young son was diagnosed with a brain tumor. When my son was sick, my life was filled with caregiving, fear, and fortitude. My family urged me to find new activities for myself. As a writer, the only thing I wanted to do was be around other writers. Bill suggested I attend one of his classes. He taught a number of writing classes. Of all his classes, he wanted me to attend the Friday morning group he led for seniors, in which all of the writers were over the age of seventy.

Bill had a special way of making everyone feel like they were his best friend. Women leaned in close when he told his stories, and the men stood tall and grinned. He marched in that first day of class wearing jeans and boots. The way he leaned on the edge of his teacher's desk exuded strength and power.

Bill pointed to a chair and motioned for me to sit down.

I slid into my seat, and my notebook fell off my lap and landed on the floor with a thump.

Each week Bill called on me in class, and I couldn't come up with an answer.

Although we were good friends, in a classroom setting it felt like I didn't know Bill at all. He gave out fiction writing homework assignments, and I didn't turn mine in. I was fully engaged; I looked forward to the classes. But I was a nonfiction writer. I wrote feature articles and penned a monthly column in a family magazine, and I wasn't having fun writing fiction.

One morning Bill walked over to me and put his hand on my shoulder.

"Do the assignments," he said, "but try writing memoir instead."

I glanced up; our eyes met. His face was filled with concern. I blushed.

I began doing my homework assignments, and memoirs tumbled out of me like clothes from a dryer opened mid-cycle.

At the end of each class, Bill selected two homework assignments to read aloud, and feedback was offered. Later there was conversation and laughter, and the mornings always ended in a way that fed my soul. Those Friday morning writing classes became the anchor in my life. They felt like a combination of quilting bee, going to sweat lodge, writing lessons, and therapy all mixed together.

I began to make friends with the women in class. Two were Native women elders I recognized from gatherings within our local Native community, but I did not know them well, not yet.

Our Native community was a mix of Chumash, with Santa Ynez Mission Band Chumash, who were recognized by the federal government, and Coastal Band Chumash, who applied for recognition in 1981. We were also blended with Native people of other tribes, including some of the unrecognized California tribes, along with undocumented Native people. Our community was fragmented the way many California tribal people are—unrecognized, without the continuity and federal recognition many other tribes have.

Too often there is a division between who is federally recognized and tribally enrolled. Yet in our Native community, most important was the fact that we were are all Indians, and we listened to the elders, they led, and we did as they instructed. We also all moved through our lives respectful of Chumash ways, and we held the history of the Chumash people in our hearts.

Other older women in the writing class, along with a couple of older men, all in their seventies and eighties, were not Native, and they understood the importance of respect for Native land and for its people. Everyone in the class had a common bond: we all lived in an area that made up the traditional Chumash homeland.

After class the women brought paper sack lunches to the park looking out over the ocean. On clear days the island of Limuw loomed in the distance. Chumash creation stories tell how Hutash, the Earth Mother, created the first Chumash people on the island of Limuw, also known as Santa Cruz Island.

The first time I gathered at the park with the women, they talked about how the female body was connected with the moon, the ocean tides, and the seasons. This was something Auntie often spoke of. Sometimes they talked about women's spiritual work and the sacredness of women in the traditional ways their grandmothers had been raised within matrilineal cultures. Except they didn't say it like that. It just flowed from brief comments they made within our conversations. Whatever it was, it gave me goose bumps, like I had when Auntie told me her stories.

Auntie's stories began in the evening, as the sun was going down. The turquoise beads she wore on Sundays made her white hair shine. Her skin was like dark, smooth clay, and when she laughed, she held her hand in front of her mouth to hide her bare gums.

Before bed, she gathered me and all of the girl cousins and reminded us to remember our dreams and to feel our feet growing up from the ground so we would be able to find our paths within the great circle in relation to how Indigenous people viewed the world.

According to Auntie, there was woman's work leading to our spiritual path. She said it was equally important to be kind and to hold space for other women as they followed their path.

The stories she told me, way back in the 1950s, spoke of the female cycles of life within the medicine world and how our feminine energy was connecting us with Grandmother Moon. But she never used those exact words. Instead, she told stories, the ones that helped Native children to understand there was a natural world and a spirit world and places connecting the two, through which some could, if they were supposed to, move from one to the other.

Except I thought her stories were like fairy tales. There is a Grandmother Spider creation story, a traditional tale, and I thought she told it to me to keep my mind off all the teasing I got at school. The kid's called me "spider." Our last name was Webb, and I had long skinny legs.

Auntie and I grew up within a family in which all of the women had known their great-grandmothers. I grew up with my great-grandmother, and she had known her great-grandmother. From her great-grandmother, Auntie learned how to dig sweet root from the ground. Yellow root, lady's slipper, she knew all of them. She knew about the helper plants. The ones that were not strong enough on their own and could help other medicine plants become stronger when combined.

"Time goes in a circle," Auntie said. Everything that has ever happened or ever will happen is going on all around me, always. I didn't understand. Yet I could feel roots beneath my feet reaching back or forward into an invisible place where time lived. I thought of it as one big swirling windy place, where all of the things that will happen in the future and what happened before I was born came together and had a meeting of sorts. I didn't know how, only that they did.

Most of the time I couldn't comprehend what Auntie was telling me, and I tucked her words into my heart for safekeeping.

After Auntie passed into the spirit world, Bill came into my life and led me into a circle of forward-thinking elders. Two of the elder women I was beginning to grow close with, Marie and Ann, were back-to the-blanket women following the feminine ways within the American Indian traditions they grew up in. They were picking up where Auntie left off.

Except I wasn't ready to carry it. I didn't understand. At first I thought Bill and the elder Native women he introduced me to were just teaching me to become a better writer.

When his health began to give out, Bill wanted to cut back. Then, at the last moment, he decided to keep his writing class going as long as he could. He turned his focus toward teaching us how to write a book. I was working on a memoir, my motherhood story.

"The theme within a book," Bill said, "is the slender golden thread that runs through the manuscript, and it comes from the idea. The flip side of the theme is the statement you are going to make." He ran his hand through his hair, smoothing it down.

"Hold those different paths the story can take. Hold the paths against the theme."

He grabbed his glasses off his face, pinched the bridge of his nose.

I looked into his red-rimmed eyes. He pointed to my notebook.

"Write it down," he said. Bill wheezed when he talked and ran out of breath.

Each week Bill asked us to read a page from our book-in-progress. When it was my turn to read, the overhead fluorescents buzzed, and my heart pounded.

"When writing memoir, you've got to show the reader who you are," Bill said.

"Don't hide racial markers."

I tensed up. My legs like a runner at the starting block. Suddenly I understood how deeply I was caught between two worlds. When I was in an all-Indian or an all-white setting, I behaved accordingly. I was either here or there. Bold enough to speak out and support Native rights and politics no matter where I was, and I never let anyone get away with ethnic slurs and racist statements. But I was a chameleon. My first impulse was to try to blend in. I thought about how my paternal grandfather covered all of the time, passing as white whenever he could. Auntie never covered. My cousins never covered, and my elder women friends never covered. I'd observed Bill acting Black with Black friends, Indian when he was with Indian friends, and white when he was with white friends. But he didn't cover. He was just doing what we all do when we are within our own ethnic group, where everyone carries the same speech tags, humor, and innuendos and has a common consciousness.

"Covering is a slippery slope," Bill said.

"Race is a necessary detail, include it."

Bill was once a bear of a man. Now he traveled on legs so shaky he appeared on the verge of collapse. His wife had died from cancer a few months earlier. He sold his house and began sorting through his possessions, deciding what to keep or give away.

He asked me to help his youngest daughter sort through his wife's clothes.

"I can't do it," I said, "Ask someone in the family. It's too personal."

Bill insisted.

I could tell his daughter didn't want me to be with her, but I also sensed she didn't want to do it alone. It was a job that must be done, and I didn't blame her for not wanting me there. What we both wanted was for her mother to be alive and to be caring for her own things.

We opened the drawers of the dresser and pulled each item out and placed it on the floor. Then we sat cross-legged, peering down at the contents. Everything was folded and smelled of laundry detergent and sachet. I said a prayer before touching any of the clothes and tried to make myself appear as small as possible, to take up little space and presence so the spirit of the woman who had owned this clothing could fill the room.

Bill's wife had dressed with that certain chic I admired in older women. Sorting through her closet was like reading a book she had written, and the fabrics told her stories. As I lifted out each item, I could tell which ones had been saved for special and the things worn daily.

Bill held a yard sale. The money earned was given to hospice. Pots and pans lined the driveway. Casserole dishes, plates, cups, and bowls that once carried his family through their lives now sat forlorn, lost and pitiful looking. Again, he assigned me to clothing. My job was to hang everything up on clothes hangers and to keep things tidy. After the beloved dresses, shirts, and sweaters had been rummaged through, I picked up the ones that had fallen onto the lawn, brushed the bits of dirt and leaves off them, and hung them back up. At the end of the day, we piled the few items left near the garage, and I covered them with a blue plastic tarp.

Bill moved into an apartment in an assisted living center. His health seemed stable enough. The last time I saw Bill alive, I said, before dashing out the door, "See you next week."

"I certainly do hope we have the chance to be together again," he said.

I didn't want to think about what Bill was saying, but I knew exactly what he meant.

I couldn't look him in the eye. It was one of those stark, intimate moments I wasn't comfortable with and didn't know how to be present in, so I brushed it off, pretended I didn't understand.

"I'm glad to see you are getting on well with Marie," Bill said.

I nodded. Sometimes Marie took over Bill's classes when he was wasn't strong enough.

Bill stared at me. "You've got an old Indian inside you. You know that, right?"

My eyes dropped to the linoleum floor. The question took me by surprise.

My face turned hot. I looked up and nodded. "Yes," I said.

"Good," Bill said, with a long sigh that was swallowed by the night.

When I received the phone call telling me Bill was dead, I looked out the window at the night sky, searching for the moon. I felt as if time, as I had always known it, had collapsed around me and it was going in a circle, just like Auntie always said it would.

2

MARIE

After Bill died, Marie began leading his classes, and she took on the role of coaxing memoirs from me. She quoted Gabriel García Márquez: "Life is not what one has lived but what one remembers and how one remembers it in order to recount it." Marie said I probably had enough lived material inside me to last a lifetime, but if I ever ran out of stories to tell, there was fiction.

I was thirty-nine when my friendship with Marie began to deepen. She was the same age as my grandmother. I was going through some hard times, and Marie opened her arms, embracing me, offering her friendship as a bridge to help lift me from grief and instruct me in living. She could see I had lost my way.

Marie had the radiant warmth and gravitational pull of a sun. She was Lakota, and in addition to her role as writer, editor, and professor of English, Marie was an ardent hiker. Before she moved to California, she lived in a variety of locations. When she lived near Santo Domingo Pueblo in the 1970s, over a course of time she became introduced to some of the tribes in and around the area whose members maintained camping grounds on their reservations, where well-behaved strangers were welcomed. Marie knew when to be quiet, and she listened well. She had a favorite reservation she liked to camp on where there were hiking trails galore.

Galore, that was one of Marie's words, and *fiddlesticks*. On days when a piece of writing was giving me a hard time, I went to Marie.

"Fiddlesticks," she said. "Let yourself listen, and instead of trying to think something up, write about what you are thinking."

When Marie spoke of writing or hiking, she pulled herself to her full height. Her frame filled the doorway, and her eyes were like two bright jewels. Her long hair was caught in a band that matched her hiking boots, and the tendrils escaping around her neck were bunched like fern curls. She stood with each foot firmly planted in front of the other. Fueled with an idea, Marie looked like she could march through solid rock. She spoke her mind, never holding back.

Then she narrowed her eyes and broke out into a wide grin. Her welcoming smile had a way of letting you know that there wasn't any place in the world she would rather be than with you in the moment.

"Since I'm Indian from my daddy's side of the family," Marie said, "it means I don't belong to a clan in my dad's tribe, because it's a matrilineal society. If only your daddy is Indian, you are thought to be born for the tribe but not into a clan with equal inheritance as a person whose Indian blood comes from their mother."

I sighed. Most American Indian tribes are matrilineal. I'm Indian from my daddy's side of the family, and this is a fact about American Indian lives that I've grown up with. It is accepted as the natural way things are, and it did not derail Marie.

Raised by her paternal grandmother, she knew who she was and was careful to make it known she wasn't speaking for, or representing, her tribe. For Native people it's important not to mislead anyone into believing they are interacting within a tribal-specific framework unless they have been given permission by the tribe.

When I spent time with Marie, I felt that just by being with her, watching and listening, I was learning to grow old in a beautiful way.

After I got to know Marie well, I learned she was walking a medicine path as her grandmother had. But she never used those words. Instead, she lived her life as an example.

She was wise enough to offer the impression she was no different than any other old woman. This is what drew me in.

3

ANN

Next, I became friendly with Ann. She might have known every Native woman in town, and I thank my lucky stars we became good friends. It could have gone either way. I first met her through Bill and Marie, but Ann was always busy, rushing off to do something, always in and out of view—until the day I was hired as a project director at American Indian Health. On my first day of my new job, I was given an office, and I set myself up to work.

Later in the afternoon, a woman came into my office and began moseying around. It was Ann. We said our howdy dos, and then she sat down in a chair and began thumbing through paperwork, making notes. After a while she asked if it was okay to use the computer. She worked for a while, and then she left.

The next afternoon she came into my office again, and we repeated the same routine. I didn't know what to make of it.

On the third day, Ann walked in and narrowed her eyes. "This is my office, and I don't mind you being here, but we need to coordinate our schedules."

I stood up, clutching my notebook against my chest.

"What are you talking about? It's my office," I said.

We went to our supervisor and discovered the office belonged to both of us. We were expected to share, but nobody had bothered to tell us ahead of time.

We had a good laugh, learned to work together, and became close friends. It was a friendship that would grow long and take me into my own elder years. Along with her work as a teacher within the public school district, many hours volunteering in the community, and her half-time job with American Indian Health, Ann was also a sought-after fiber artist and painter, and she taught basket weaving, beading, pottery, and Native crafts to children and adults.

She had given birth to two children and had adopted two more. Now she was a grandmother. Ann was a terrible housekeeper and an extremely good teacher, friend, artist, and storyteller. She was also easily distracted. All the time I reminded her what she was forgetting. Where are your keys? Your glasses? The bag of basket weaving and beadwork you brought in from the car? Yet her mind was knife sharp. The important things she needed to remember were never forgotten.

I have no idea how old Ann was when we first met. She seemed ageless, with dancing dark eyes, and she was filled with stories, her own stories, and she retold traditional Native stories. The oral tradition, the teaching stories that guide us from the mundane to the spirit world. Her words flowed through the room, around the campfire, floating in the air, the impact of her words streaming down faces. I saw her voice.

Ann was Gabrielino-Tongva. A California Indian tribe also known as the San Gabriel Band of Mission Indians. She remembers how her tribe was called the "diggers" in the 1950s, and if you wanted to be treated nice by white people, it was best if you could find a way to not let them know you were Indian, certainly not a digger. For Ann, being Indian took place only at home, with family, where it was safe.

During the Native Renaissance of the 1960s, Ann emerged as a proud, card-carrying Indian, tribally enrolled, carrying the traditions of her tribe, and doing important work within California Indian Country.

Ann introduced me to the plants that make good basketry materials. She held out a stalk of deer grass for me to examine. "When immersed in water, baskets made with flowering culms become watertight as the stalk expands, making them perfect for water jugs and cooking baskets." She knew how Indians used wild plants for food, medicine, and crafts and about the plants used to make natural dyes and which ones were gathered from below sea level or above timberline.

Ann gave off no pretense. She was wise enough to offer the impression she was no different than any other older woman with a strong connection to the natural world.

4

IRENE

One afternoon a woman walked into the office I shared with Ann at Indian Health. She sat down on the stool across from me and laced her fingers together and leaned back against the wall.

"Did Ann tell you about me?" she asked.

Before I got a chance to answer, she pulled a package of ginger snaps out of her handbag, offered me a cookie, and grinned. "I'm Irene. Chippewa." She shrugged. "Did Ann tell you I'm going along with you to the conference next weekend?"

At seventy-five, with her tight jeans, blue-black hair, and flirty personality, Irene reminded me so much of my aunt Jo (Auntie's younger sister). I had to keep reminding myself that she wasn't my aunt Josephine.

The day we traveled together to the Native women's conference, I held my breath to keep from laughing out loud as we boarded the airplane because Irene's beaded tobacco pouch was swinging from her neck while she carried on with whoever happened to be near us. On the plane her chatter never slowed, with everyone around us listening and watching and me smiling. Men liked her; she made them laugh.

Frequently, I went to powwows with Ann and Irene. Irene didn't drive. Being the youngest, I knew it was my responsibility to offer to drive. But I drive the speed limit, and Ann didn't like to poke along the highway. So, she always drove her car, which is basically a mini California Indian Country, filled with regalia, camping gear, fixings for frybread tacos, basket weaving supplies, beadwork projects, blankets for giveaways, and a string of small abalone shells swinging from the rearview mirror.

In those days I drank Dr. Pepper so I could keep up with Irene, dancing long after the moon was full, wearing moccasins beaded in colors of sunrise, clouds, and blue skies, her buckskin dress swaying. Irene danced the powwow competitions, women's buckskin style, northern, in the golden age category. Her movements were smooth and flowing. Carrying her fringed shawl over one arm, her shoulders swayed gently, and sunlight played against her fully beaded cape. Native regalia is imbued with spiritual meaning and is an expression of culture and identity. For Native dancers, not only is the act of dancing that expression, but the wearing of dance regalia is also a visible manifestation of one's heritage. Often the beadwork contains personal motifs that reflect the dancer's tribe, and beadwork is frequently created by a family member and given as a gift to the dancer.

Late at night, after she had changed her clothes, with her social dance shawl draped over her shoulders, Irene loved to tell us stories about when she was nineteen and had been chosen as head girl dancer.

"It was a great honor, and I felt like queen of the powwow that weekend," she said.

Her eyes lit up like two high-beam headlights lighting up a dark mountain road when she told us about her younger days of dancing, and I was fond of listening.

Powwow is a modern-day word. Before the First World War, they were called gatherings. After the corn was all dried, pumpkins sliced, and the wild plums brought in, it was a time for giving thanks. When the food was together for the hard winter months and when the work was all done, they gathered. After World War I these gatherings were held to honor those servicemen who came back.

Today a powwow is an intertribal event celebrating being Indian and pride in American Indians. It's also a reunion for many Native families, clans, and tribes spread apart in different cities or reservations. There is the exchange of news, ideas, song and dance, and Native fashion, style, and art. It provides the opportunity for hearing and the sharing of a variety of tribal languages spoken, upholding tribal customs, and it's a time when Native people reflect on traditions.

The term *powwow* derives from the Algonquian Indian word *pau wau*, which means "he dreams." Early powwows were an all-Indian event. Today the contemporary powwow is frequently open to the public. The concept of the powwow originated among the tribes that inhabited the Great Plains from the southern prairies of Canada to the lower plains of Texas. In the era before reservations, many Plains Indian tribes formed intertribal alliances. These alliances allowed tribe-specific songs, dances, and ceremonies to be exchanged, and in this way the "intertribal powwow" as we know it today emerged.

Irene said the first intertribal powwow was held in Oklahoma and is remembered as the Ponca Powwow in northern Indian Territory around 1880. Back in those days, all of Indian Territory was intertribal because at least sixty-seven tribes were historically associated with the land that later became Oklahoma.

It was as if Irene had been born for powwow life. While dancing in the arena, she was transported back into the old days. But when she wasn't dancing, Irene liked to have a good time. She was free-spirited, and I suspected she had been very promiscuous in her younger days. When I was with Irene and Ann, it brought out the free-spirited, promiscuous side of me. I felt uninhibited, spontaneous, and most of all I trusted my instincts. It was the way I was before I worked so hard to clean myself up and become overly responsible. While I never got into any serious trouble while growing up, I felt that I'd wasted my youth with too many parties, too many boys, and not reaching enough of my goals. By the time I was thirty, I was determined to work hard to make up for the time I felt I'd lost. I had become so serious and responsible that casual friends who did not know me well made comments suggesting they thought that I had been the kind of girl who followed all of the rules, didn't drink or smoke, a clean-cut, well-behaving, timid, mainstream, conservative, good girl. This let me know I had cleaned myself up too much and my spirit was now hidden.

When I was with Irene and Ann at a powwow, we always behaved in a respectful manner around elders, and when we were inside, or near the arena, we behaved respectfully. But when we were alone, we were playful and sometimes downright rowdy.

I sensed that Irene might have been one of those girls in high school with a bad reputation. In my mind I could see her stumble out of a van at dawn, wearing drugstore flip-flops, clothes rumpled, hair tacky, and breath all cigarettes and yesterday's wine.

Now Irene was a longtime member of Alcoholics Anonymous, and she had quit smoking. But she still painted her nails high-alert red—her color—and it matched her powwow shawl, the one she wore for social dances.

When I was at a powwow with Irene and Ann, we were returned to girls, sixteen, looking for our fun. Irene pointed to an old man with long gray hair pulled into a low ponytail. A grass dancer, but he had taken off his regalia and was wearing jeans and a flannel shirt. Irene turned to me grinning, leaned forward in her chair, and swung her feet to the ground. She walked over to the man. Her voice was lilting. "I'm Irene," she said. She smiled, her eyes brown, dreamy, and giant. The man tipped his hat and put his hand on Irene's back, just above her hips.

Often, I could expect impish, playful days with Irene. Yet I also had to tiptoe around her moods. She held grudges and allowed anger to rule. But most of all I loved to watch Irene flirt.

5

MARY LOU

One friendship led to another, and my circle of elder women friends began to grow. Friendship with Bill and Marie led me to Mary Lou. She was one of the best writers in Bill's class, and she offered the best feedback. She knew how to help make my stories stronger by telling me what I was doing right. Then she pointed to the places needing further work and offered suggestions.

Once an actor and a dancer, she had danced with a theater company in New York. Twice married, each time to an actor. She described herself as pretty as early morning in her youth. Mary Lou was beautiful at eighty. She lived with two cats and worked as a writer.

We'd stroll to a beachside café and order breakfast burritos for lunch and talk about writing and the men in her life and the man in mine.

Once, she shared intimate details on lovemaking and coached me on what I could expect of my body when I reached eighty. Listening to her silvery words, I got that embarrassed feeling, like I do when I see a man laughing and talking with a crowd of people and his zipper is down.

Mary Lou continued talking, and I looked away. Looked into the light filtering through the cluster of bougainvillea, fluorescent pink and magenta. I blinked then lowered my eyes and stared at my burrito.

"Get your clothes back on now," Mary Lou said. She smiled and laid her hand on mine. "Here's what else you want to hear: With older sexuality, withhold your body, too, and keep to yourself at times." Her voice ended on a low, mellow note that sounded peaceful. She smiled again and gave me a look. Her eyes were lovely, clear, like a young woman's eyes.

Mary Lou grew up in Albuquerque, and I could always get her to tell me long stories about the land in New Mexico back in the days before the cities filled up, back when the landscape was wild and free. She came of age in America in an era when nobody ever pretended to be Indian.

Mary Lou shook her head. "Some light-skinned mixed folks pretended they didn't have any Indian blood. But no one ever pretended they did."

When I asked about her ethnicity, she waved me off.

"Mixed," she said. "I have my suspicions, but if I have Indian blood, they forgot to tell me about it. And I don't ever use the word *hybrid*. I don't like that word because it denotes a selective breeding program or experiment." Her brow furrowed. "I'm just a person of mixed parentage—a mongrel."

Mary Lou was petite, with graceful wrinkled arms, a dancer's body, aged, and had reached her period of mastery; she had become something on the order of a sage. She did not view herself as a wise woman. But she had all of the qualities. Having reached the fullness of her age, Mary Lou had developed true wisdom and applied it to every area in her life. She listened to what I had to say without judgment. When she wanted to prod me into considering seeing things from another point of view, she spoke her mind thoughtfully. She was humble, her confidence had ripened and deepened, and her sense of humor was at its peak.

She taught me to love myself, to laugh at myself, and to let down my guard.

"See you next week," Mary Lou always said cheerfully at the end of our visits.

"And if I don't, remind me."

6

BACK IN THOSE DAYS

Although I was the youngest by many years, when I was with Marie, Anne, Mary Lou, and Irene, our age differences didn't matter. Circumstance had placed us on separate points on the same path. With each in a different way, I shared a common bond.

With Marie, Ann, and Irene, I gained a deeper understanding of what it means to be an urban American Indian woman. We were city Indians, living lifestyles the way most city dwellers do. Working our jobs in the community, grocery shopping, going to the library or to the movies, volunteering, and doing the variety of things most people who live in the city take part in while also moving through our lives with traditional ways of thinking and being, prayer, ceremony, and Native community connection.

Too often, doctor appointments, waiting for the plumber, our work schedules, my busy family life with my children, and all of us meeting life's demands prevented us from our Friday afternoon picnics at the park. Instead, we began gathering for lunch whenever we could. We met at the park or at the beach in warm weather, and sometimes we alternated houses. Marie lived in a rural area. When we met at her house, we sat outside at a wooden picnic table overlooking a creek. In the heat of summer, we pulled out the aluminum folding chairs and sat on the shady side of the house.

I lived near the foothills, and my house backed up to a dry creek bed surrounded by oak and eucalyptus trees, with the ocean three miles away. When an offshore breeze blew, it brought the scent of salty sea air. When we gathered at my house, we sat around the big table in my kitchen with the back door open and my dog lounging near our feet under the table.

None of our homes were fancy, but we all lived in ways that felt comfortable to us. It's a common trait for many urban Native women to have amenities we can afford and enjoy that improve our lives and not to bother with any of the extras that seem unimportant. We all had washing machines, televisions, coffee makers, microwave ovens, and more. But I didn't have a dishwasher because it wasn't important to me, and Marie didn't have a clothes dryer because she liked to use her backyard clothesline.

There is an old saying, although I don't know who said it first, that American Indians keep our old ways alive while taking on anything new from modern society that proves useful to us and discarding what is not. If something improved our lives, like computers and cell phones, we used it. But if something did not make our lives better, we always went back to our old ways.

None of us had grown up with a lot of affluence, and it didn't matter to us. We replaced the roof when the time came, painted the house, and kept things in good repair. Yet none of us had ever remodeled anything. For many Native people, to be wealthy is not to have; to be wealthy is to give.

Our lunch gatherings were made of an everybody-bring-something meal. Marie made homemade tortillas and salsa. Ann had a special way she made cornbread. Mary Lou was famous for her deviled eggs. And I'm a good soup and bean cook. Often my friends requested my pinquito beans. I soaked whole beans overnight, then simmered them on the back of the stove for hours and added a hot New Mexico chili powder, cumin, onion, and garlic. But sometimes I refried pinto beans in bacon grease, and everyone ate more than usual.

When Marie didn't have the energy to make her special salsa, I made my California beach style salsa. I called it beach style because it's not authentic in the way Marie's recipe was, handed down from her grandmother. Though I did burn and scrape my chilies.

For me the heart of the matter were the years when my young son was sick with cancer and a brain tumor, and I couldn't stretch wide enough to cover all that needed doing. In those days my friends did my share of the work. Now I gave too many favors, knowing one day I may again need to be kept afloat. Keeping the old neighborhood tradition of women gathering is the element that gave a small-town community feeling to my urban city life. Embraced within the circle of older women, we ate, talked, joked, and managed the serious and trivial aspects of womanhood together.

Ann and Irene had raised kids, and we were all raising dogs and cats. Marie and Ann had earned multiple degrees, and they were both teachers with impressive credentials, whereas I was trying to make up for my educational lack by doing serious hard work. Mary Lou and Irene were confident, free-spirited, accomplished dancers. When I was with any of these women, I could say something bold and ridiculous and not be embarrassed. They made me strive to be a better friend and a better person.

Instead of searching for a mirror image and to find friends who were similar to me, as I had done in the past, now I was drawn to women whom I perceived to be different from me, women who would have intimidated me or made me uncomfortable in a previous time of my life. There was a time when I thought it necessary to have a lot in common with a person in order for friendship to grow.

Turned out it had more to do with my own growth and ability to reach out without having expectations. I had always clung to the notion of having a best friend. One special woman to share a central core friendship, to laugh with, someone to tell me the truth even when it was hard to listen, a relationship soldered with compatibility strong enough to withstand the grit and discomforts that are also indicators of closeness.

Friendship with men came easily to me. But when I reached out to women, often it did not progress beyond a casual friendship, and it left me wondering what I was doing wrong.

I figured it had something to do with the fact that I am a loner and a person who sometimes becomes reticent. I enjoy people, and often

I'm very talkative and outgoing. But I have an extroverted personality prone to episodes when I need to be alone and silent. During those periods I'm not in a bad mood or depressed. It's more of a reserved feeling of needing to slow down, and I become quieter than usual. When this reticent feeling pulls me inward, too often people assume that I'm upset about something or that I'm mad at them. I've learned to speak right up and reassure them that nothing is wrong. Except I can tell that sometimes they don't believe me.

When I explained this to Mary Lou, she touched my cheek and said, "Maybe your reticence has something to do with the moon position you were born into, and perhaps you feel pulled into a dreaming state of mind, and that's when you want to slip away from people and be alone."

"Darling," Mary Lou cried out, exaggerating her voice, "your instinctive tendency to hold back and be a loner is part of who you are as an artist and as important as your innate predisposition to be outgoing and easygoing." I stared at her. She put out her hand. "It's all right."

I unlaced my fingers and placed a hand in Mary Lou's outstretched palm.

Being seen as a dreaming artist left me feeling warm inside, like the sun had come out bright again after slipping behind a dark cloud and the warmth had managed to slide under my skin. Usually, those who are close to me say they find the reticent side of my personality confusing.

Marie, a meticulous observer, walked over to me and put her arm on my sleeve.

"Build alone time into your daily life and look forward to it, instead of withdrawing."

For a moment I was quiet. I smiled and looked down at the dark grass by my feet. When I looked up, Marie winked at me.

"When you feel the need to slip away, just say that you have a great idea and need to go write for a few hours. Doesn't matter if you really don't want to write, just go off and do whatever helps you feel restored." Marie tilted her head to one side, and her salt-and-pepper hair swung around her rosy face.

7

RETURNING THE GIFT

July 1992. The first North American Native Writers' Festival, Returning the Gift, was taking place in Norman, Oklahoma. It was bringing more Native writers together in one place than at any other time in history, and I was in a glum mood. I'd planned to attend but had decided to stay home because my son was having trouble with his shunt. A shunt had been surgically inserted because hydrocephalus from the brain tumor persisted after surgery. He would need the shunt for the rest of his life. Usually, the shunt didn't cause him any problems. But lately he had begun having headaches, and we needed to keep a close eye on him.

I was deeply thankful Returning the Gift was taking place and that history was being made, and I was willing myself not to feel jealous for missing out. But I just couldn't shake off my disappointment, even though I knew I'd made the right decision by staying home.

The mainstream in America had reached a place where literature had turned toward multiculturalism. It was beginning to be noticed that Native literature had much in common with Asian American and African American literature. And it had a lot in common with the work of Spanish-speaking Americans, many with Native roots. The "half-breed perspective" was central to a number of powerful contemporary Native writers who found themselves balanced between cultures. This was a strong theme for many of the Native writers presenting at the Returning the Gift festival.

As a writer I was publishing within a number of mainstream, white-dominated, family-centered magazines. In addition to writing feature articles, I also wrote a monthly magazine column; my personal essays needed to show a parenting challenge I'd faced and how I solved it. I was struggling because an editor at the magazine frequently edited my writing with a decidedly white slant by changing or omitting any details showing my family was of color. The day I opened the glossy magazine and found my byline and an overedited article not sounding like anything I would ever write, with a stock photo of a white family accompanying the piece, was the day I changed my direction. I began writing personal essays with Native themes and submitting them to Native publications and literary magazines.

Early on, some of my pieces were published. Soon after, I made a connection with a Native writer who became my friend, and he led me to other Native writers. Some served as mentors while I wrote my way into becoming an emerging Native writer.

My friend frequently called, checking on me. The phone calls began when my son got sick, and he was making sure I was writing and sending my work out. He'd phone to let me know about calls for submissions. He was like Bill in that he gave his time to many people and had mentored hundreds of emerging Native writers, and through a mutual friend, he found me. He telephoned one day, out of the blue. After that, a pattern was established: at least once a month I could count on receiving a phone call and a writing pep talk from him. While I was at home, being where I needed to be, he was at Returning the Gift, in Oklahoma.

Within three decades some of the Native writers he introduced me to would become close friends, and our work would be included together in a number of anthologies published by university presses. But I didn't know any of this in 1992, and I felt alone, struggling, feeling like I had one foot in Native American literature and the other foot in the world of doctors and hospitals, while my son was recovering from a brain tumor.

8

THE SEVEN WAYS

It was about a half past nine when Marie dropped by. Her visit caught me by surprise.

She wrote in the morning hours and was protective of her time.

Marie narrowed her eyes. "I'm worried about you. My grandmother lived her life according to seven ways, or 'the ways,' as she called them. Indigenous values that guided her attitude and actions. It has helped me get through my hard years, and I think it might help you."

She put her hand on my arm. "I can't teach you the same as my grandmother taught me. But I'd like to share some of what she taught. Do you mind?"

I smiled. "I'm interested."

"Okay. Can you come over tomorrow afternoon, at two?"

I nodded.

She walked to her car, and when she got there, she stopped.

"This is not how I usually do things," she said.

"It's not?" I walked toward her.

"Usually, I don't talk about any of this." Marie blinked for a moment and stared at me. "Well, I have with my niece but usually not with anyone other than family. But I can see you need some help getting to where you need to go."

The following day, before I went to Marie's house, I put on a favorite skirt that fell just above my ankles, patterned in soft earth-toned colors. At some point while I was growing up, I'd learned that in order to show respect, it was important for older girls and women to wear a long skirt when spending time with traditional Indian women who were elders. I have no memory of who taught this to me—though most of the Native women I've known throughout my life were aware of this custom, and many followed it. Frequently, I wore a long skirt at Native community events, and I always wore a long skirt for ceremonies. But usually, I wore jeans when I was with Marie or a knee-length skirt because she treated me as her equal, made it clear we were close friends and that the atmosphere was casual, relaxed.

This day felt different. I wanted to show my respect.

When I arrived, Marie greeted me at the door, and we walked to the far end of her backyard, near her plum tree, in a patch of shade where there were two lawn chairs.

I sat up straight.

Marie took off her glasses. Color rose to her cheeks.

"Well, I'm not sure where to begin," Marie explained.

"Native people have paths they walk to learn spiritual discipline. Each tribe has their own way, according to their traditional beliefs and tribal ways. The Lakota call it "Walking in a Sacred Manner." The Diné say, "Walk in Beauty." These are only two examples. However, all tribes have their own ways and values they live by that teach them to make spiritual discipline a way of life."

"We say we are walking the ways because we are on our walk on earth while we are alive, in human form."

Marie paused. "Well, all of the Native people I grew up with refer to being alive on earth as our walk, and when we die, we have finished our walk, and we walk on."

I nodded. "Yes, that's what I was taught too."

"My grandmother," Marie said, "was guided by her tribal beliefs to live by seven values, or "the ways," as she called it, to learn to walk in humility, walk in gratitude, with respect, with caring, with compassion, with honesty, and with generosity."

Marie's eyebrows knitted together. She looked like she was about to say something and then changed her mind. Then she continued on in an endless stream of calm.

"Let's begin with seven stages of life for women that are as ancient as the human race. Growing up as a daughter. Womanhood, motherhood, gathering and learning rituals, walking the way of the teacher within the community, and elderhood. However, these stages of life are lived differently for every culture. For those of us who are Indigenous, for Native women, we live within each stage of our life following the beliefs, values, and customs of our tribe."

"What?" I said. "But I'm a combination of three tribes, and I didn't grow up within a traditional community in any of my tribes."

I wrinkled my brow. "My aunt used to tell me some of the medicine stories passed down from her great-grandmother, but I didn't understand them."

"Shhh," Marie said. Her voice was soft, gentle.

She took a deep breath. "Native literature, composed of U.S. western literary tradition, is packed into the hyphens of the oral tradition, so it's important for you to read and learn as much as you can about the creation and traditional teaching stories."

I nodded again, crossed my arms, and slumped back in my chair. I was hoping for a more intimate response. I wanted Marie to delve deeper.

Marie's eyes widened. She was silent for a few minutes.

"The first thing you need to understand is that while we are in each phase of our life, we continue learning the seven values, and how we learn plays out according to what is going on in our life in each stage of our life."

The wind picked up, blowing leaves around the yard. Marie kept her eyes on me.

"You are walking in womanhood now, but let's start at the beginning. When you were born, you became a daughter. Your growing-up years were spent gathering experiences. Ideally, your mother, grandmother, aunties, those who raised you, began to teach you in a manner that would help you begin to gain humility, gratitude, respect, caring, compassion, honesty, generosity.

"If you had been my granddaughter, I would have also kept an eye out to discover what you enjoyed. Your strengths. Your weaknesses. The gifts you brought to this lifetime. All along I would be guiding you to help you find yourself, find your path, as you walked the way of the daughter."

Marie laced her fingers together and leaned back in her chair.

"Womanhood is where you are now. The years when a woman develops self-reliance, manages a household, and learns to manage an independent life in the adult world. You are taking the journey as a writer, and it's leading you on your spiritual path, but if you had not yet found your path, I would help you. I'd steer you toward different types of work and volunteering. But remember, it's important to stay open, a woman will have many callings, and often our callings have beginnings and endings taking us to unexpected places."

I wondered where all this was leading. I took my eyes off Marie for a moment and looked at the plum tree. The air was thickly scented with the smell of growing things. Plums, tomatoes, berries, butterflies, birds, all vied for my attention.

Marie looked up. She blinked. "Motherhood is a path many women walk. This is when a woman learns the discipline of much sacrifice. Her body, her time, her social life, and her relationships. Everything is called upon while she is raising her children. This stage of life pushes a woman to stretch and use all of her capabilities."

Marie glanced at me. "But a woman does not have to give birth to children or even have children in order to learn the lessons on this path. Caring for children, working as a teacher or in any capacity dedicated to children, is a form of mothering.

"Gathering and learning rituals are ways of walking for many Native women, and it's also an ancient way walked by woman all over the world. Gathering applies to gathering knowledge, along with harvesting and gathering food sources, plants and herbs for healing, reeds for basket weaving, and gaining a knowledge of the seasons. During this stage of life, we develop a stronger sense of ourselves. The most important spiritual law is that we must always give before we take anything, and what we take, whenever possible, should be used to further and nurture life.

"Walking the way of the teacher often comes after years of learning, experiencing, and nurturing, volunteering. We are then ready to share the skills, stories, and wisdom we have gained. This might mean evolving to healing or going into politics or public service. This is a time for leadership. We also give our time to grandchildren and great-grandchildren and to other children in the community. It's a time of serving as a mentor and role model for younger woman.

"Everyone will grow old, yet in order to attain elderhood in a wise manner, in many cultures, including Native cultures, it is necessary to do our best to learn to master the seven values. If we live our lives always practicing the seven values, we have the opportunity to gain wisdom."

Marie glanced over at me just then. When I caught her eye, she looked away.

"The way of the medicine woman begins early in life, and after a woman has reached the fullness of her age in elderhood, the path deepens."

I wrinkled my nose.

"The seven ways is not only for women on a shamanic path." Marie explained. "Walking in a sacred manner yields increased spiritual awareness."

I nodded again, like a good student, and she exhaled.

"You need someone to nudge you in that direction."

I knew what Marie was saying. We all need teachers in our lives. I was looking for more writing teachers. I wanted to follow the way of the writer.

We sat quietly for a moment. Marie glanced over at me.

"You can sit back and grow old and become elderly. Or you can pay attention and do what is needed to grow right as an elder."

I shook my head and said nothing. But Marie had already picked up on my hesitation.

"A spiritual life manifests in the day-to-day world. If you keep your mind too wrapped up worrying and distracted by all of the millions of things we all must do just to keep going, you won't develop spiritual awareness."

I looked down at my hands, then up at Marie.

"But I didn't grow up in a tribe. Aren't these teachings supposed to be taught within a tribal framework by an elder within the tribe?" I asked.

"That's the best way," Marie said, "but if it was the only way to learn, it would mean that those who are tribally enrolled but did not grow up on their reservation might not have the opportunity to learn from a tribal elder."

She fixed her eyes on me. "There are also a great many Indian people who are undocumented, not tribally enrolled, and most of them will likely never have an opportunity to learn from a tribal elder."

"Some Native people learn from their mothers and grandmothers. But often the path is cut short when the mother or grandmother dies, walks on. Then another woman will take over and teach the girl what she needs to know."

Marie shook her head. "And what about the babies who are removed from their homes and placed with parents in other tribes or with white parents and not given the chance to grow up with their Native culture?"

"But if I'm not following a tribal framework from either of the tribes I'm descended from," I faltered, "how will I be guided in an Indigenous way?"

I knew better than to think Native beliefs were ecumenical and interchangeable, and I was always searching for commonalities within Cherokee, Lenape, and Seneca ways and beliefs.

In order to be authentic, I wanted to feel a bridge of connection without implying anything that might be viewed as intertribal homogeneity.

Marie's eyes searched my face as if she could read my thoughts.

"All tribes and Nations have different cultural beliefs, but there are a few things we all share. In traditional indigenous communities, there is an understanding that our lives play themselves out within a set of reciprocal relationships."

Marie smiled. She leaned toward me.

"Look inside yourself, trust your own thinking, and believe in your own power. What you are searching for to guide you is asleep within you, and if you weave these seven values and ways into your everyday life, your intuition will wake up."

Marie stood up and walked over to where I was sitting. She placed her hand on my shoulder.

"There is nothing wrong with learning about spiritual awareness informally. Even if I wanted to, I couldn't begin to teach you the traditional ways my grandmother taught me from her tribal upbringing. The way I learned begins very early in life."

I nodded.

Staring into my face, Marie said. "But you can begin to live your life by upholding the seven values, and by folding them into your life, you can begin walking these seven ways. You can start right away, beginning in this moment."

The wind picked up again. All around us leaves were tossing.

"Walking the ways won't be hard," Marie said. "All you need to do is start paying attention and stay alert. You will be living and thinking in a manner that is almost, but not quite, the same as you are used to." Marie flashed me a quick smile. "You'll see."

I froze for a moment, and everything went silent. The birds stopped singing their songs. The wind stopped. The water in the creek behind where we were sitting stopped gurgling and fell still, and I could feel my heart racing. I could see where this was leading. I would have the same social life but would need to do more Native community volunteering. I didn't always accept responsibility for my own shortcomings. I'd need to stop blaming others and allowing their actions to hold me back.

A part of me was glad to be nudged into being accountable for my thoughts and emotions. Still, the room started to spin when I realized that I would need to engage continually in mindful thinking, behavior, and awareness as a way of life. It was a path I would walk every moment, even when I was asleep.

Then I thought about how Ann had begun to take me in, giving great amounts of her time guiding me. She was teaching me what I needed to know to be helpful and mindful within the Tongva ways for women and to better understand California Indians. When I was with Ann, I felt as if I was in training to learn to walk in balance within her Indigenous way. Then it occurred to me that I *was* being trained.

And Mary Lou? All along she had been gently guiding me. Not as a Native elder. Yet everything she said and did was proof she had mastered the seven values and had attained elderhood with much wisdom.

My voice quivered in my throat. I looked into Marie's dark eyes.

"All right," I said. "I'll do it."

I chuckled. "Might as well agree since I've been doing it for a while now, stumbling along without knowing there was a path."

I could feel the blood rushing to my head. The big difference would be that now when I was being lazy, not wanting to take responsibility, not pulling my weight, or lying to myself, I would have to admit it to myself and step up.

I could see why Marie had explained the seven ways to me beginning with childhood, moving into adulthood, older age, and then elderhood. I visualized the female cycles of life unfolding in a linear direction. I wanted them to line up in an orderly fashion, with a lesson plan to follow. But then I remembered something Auntie talked about and what Indigenous people have always known: time is not linear; time is cyclical.

In some traditional Native languages, there is no word to describe time as it is defined by Western science. Learning to uphold the seven values would be walked in a cyclical manner. There would be movement followed by stillness. Confusion. Clarity. Everything in constant flux and continuous motion without a clear line defining where one way ended and another began. Most of all, nothing would really ever end; it would go in a circle.

When I asked Marie more questions, she was quiet for a long time. I could not hear what she said next. Her voice was soft, and the wind whipped the words out of her mouth. My instincts told me I should be quiet and not ask more questions. There are certain teachings and sacred knowledge from all Indigenous cultures and within all tribes that should never be talked about—or written. These things should only be passed on orally when the time is right and sometimes never at all.

Native America does not function in the same manner or from the same assumptions Western systems do. Marie was not offering to be my life coach. We would not meet weekly to talk about my feelings or discuss ways for me to attain greater fulfillment or come up with strategies for overcoming obstacles. That would be my job, for me to figure out.

Marie was also not taking on the role as my spiritual leader. She was only teaching me what I needed to know to make myself ready. To prepare me for elderhood in the years ahead and for a time when I might begin further learning from other elders.

From the lessons Auntie taught, I knew this would be my own private journey. The twists and turns, the good things and difficulties in my life, would provide me with plenty of opportunities to learn to walk with humility, gratitude, respect, caring, compassion, honesty, and generosity, and hopefully, I would gain some wisdom.

These lessons and opportunities would come from the events and things that happened in my life, to give me a chance to stretch, reach deeper. With each event that occurred, I had the choice to grumble and complain, to blame others, to make excuses. Or I could begin to see that I had been invited. Called forth to view obstacles as an opportunity to grow and change in positive ways.

Marie would offer instruction from time to time. But I would need to pay careful attention because it would not happen within ordinary conversation. I would be shown and would find myself in situations that offered me an opportunity to grow personally and spiritually.

This is exactly what Ann and Mary Lou had been doing for a while now, and I knew they would continue to guide me. I would need to use my best listening skills and be aware.

Marie, Ann, and Mary Lou were raising me up and guiding me, the way Auntie would have done. Like women all over the world, I had walked the way of the daughter, walked into womanhood and motherhood, without being aware I was already on the path.

I knew that only certain girls and young women chosen and specifically guided by trained elders within the tribe would be summoned to walk the traditional path of medicine woman, and I had not been selected for this purpose. Nor did I want to be selected. I had no desire to aspire to medicine woman. But I did want to grow right as an elder.

I began to understand that paying attention, staying alert and learning to grow mindful, was helpful for any woman. Reminders to walk in a sacred manner, to walk gently, to walk in beauty and in balance, were exactly what I needed.

I could hear Auntie's voice in my mind. "The moment we let the spiritual world know we are open to learning, opportunity will arrive, and the teachers and lessons won't be the ones you are expecting to find." Her words sounded like wind shaking the leaves on a tree.

9

THE WAY OF THIS DAUGHTER

My mother turned sixteen two weeks after I was born. She was raised in a white, working-class, devout Christian family, with a mother who was too strict, rigid, and uncompromising. My grandmother needed things her way, and she was unyielding. Mom's father was gentle and kind. But he allowed my grandmother to be in charge, and my mom fought against the harsh rules her mother forced the family to follow. She rebelled by dating a rabble-rousing, rough-around-the-edges American Indian boy. That boy became my father.

My dad was seventeen when my mom got pregnant. When I was born, in 1953, he was a high school dropout, employed full-time as a box boy at a grocery store.

His extended relatives of aunties, uncles, and cousins were kind-hearted. But his father was mean. He hurled insults and was abusive, and my dad's mother cried often. Before they divorced, his mother had a breakdown, and she neglected my dad. He left his sorry home life behind when he was sixteen, and he lived in his car or slept on the couch at a friend's house while dating my mother.

My dad grew up in a large, tight-knit family from Oklahoma. His father was Cherokee, Lenape, and Seneca, with some Black and white ancestry mixed in. His father's family is descended from the Indian people who stayed behind after the passage of the Indian Removal Act in 1830, when tens of thousands of American Indians were relocated from the American Southeast.

Exile came immediately after the Indian Removal Bill became law. Indians were rounded up and left with only what they could carry. It was followed by removal treaties with the tribes. The five large tribes—Cherokee, Chickasaw, Choctaw, Creek, and Seminole—and many smaller tribes in the region had already been greatly reduced in population and land base. Some of the smaller tribes in the area were already amalgamated with the larger tribes by the time of removal. For Indian people in the South, it meant exile to lands west of the Mississippi River. However, a substantial Indian population remained behind after those massive relocations.

In 1830, when President Jackson signed the Indian Removal Act, his intention was for every Indian in the Southeast to be removed and to have the land vacated so that a new era of occupation would open up for white Americans in the Southeast. However, many Indian people found ways to remain in their homelands. A great number hid out in the hills, continuing on. Others began living in small Indian communities and remained separate from larger groups of Indians, with varying degrees of acculturation, accommodating to the Black and white societies around them.

The end of the Civil War allowed white American settlements into the West, and many tribal nations were pressed onto reservations in the Indian Territory. In 1867 many tribes living in Kansas and Nebraska received new reservations by the Omnibus Treaty. The Plains nations accepted reservations by the Medicine Lodge Treaty.

With many tribes removed and relocated, my Cherokee and Lenape ancestors came to live adjacent to each other in Indian Territory, and eventually intermarriage of very unlike tribal peoples became normalized.

I don't know what year my dad's family traveled to Indian Territory, but they arrived desperately poor, and for generations the poverty in our family continued. When my grandfather and his siblings, including Auntie, were growing up, the family sharecropped, moving from one farm to another.

After the Great Dust Bowl, my grandfather came to California with his oldest brother. Auntie came a few years later, and some of her younger siblings followed. Other family members stayed in Oklahoma. Eventually, my great-grandparents came to California, and when they arrived, they moved into a circus tent. My dad remembers Grandma's black stove was in the center of the tent, with the stove pipe poking out through the center. As a boy, for fun, my dad crawled in and out of the tent flaps in the places where the wind whipped in. In Oklahoma the family lived without running water and electricity, so a circus tent made a good home for them to start out in.

When I was young, my great-grandparents moved into a house, and every Sunday we spent the entire day with them. We'd arrive mid-morning and stay after dinner, until the night began to grow late. I never thought of them as my great-grandparents. To me they were just my grandma and grandpa. My dad's father was also always around on Sundays, but I'd grown up calling him Papa, so there was never any confusion.

My mom didn't like to spend Sundays with my dad's family, but for me it was the center of the universe. The house was always filled with relatives. The cousins all played together like a pack of wild pups. Grandpa, Papa, and the uncles talked politics, shouting out their rock-bottom opinions, while Grandma, the aunties, and my older girl cousins gossiped, with me listening in.

Nobody ever went away without eating. Grandma could cook a meal to feed fifteen of us. I loved to sit with my feet on the fender of her coal-black stove, listening to the stories Auntie told while the women cooked together in the kitchen. Grandma talked about the old days in Oklahoma, when the prairie was covered with buffalo grass that rippled and changed color when the wind blew on it. I loved to listen. Her stories allowed me to glimpse pictures of a world unknown to me.

Although my dad didn't play an instrument, he was raised in the mixed-blood fiddle tradition, and I grew up listening. The uncles played the fiddle, banjo, and guitar, and Grandma played the harmonica. She took out her teeth and dropped them into her apron pocket before she started playing. She could step dance too, but back then we called it dancing the jig.

The mixed-blood fiddle tradition reflects that we are a mixed people of Native and other heritages, and the music defines who mixed-bloods are, a blend of Native and European descents, and when the white and Indian cultures collided, the music collided. Within the fiddle music, you can hear the drumbeat of our Native American style of fiddling, blended with the fiddle music from Scotland, Ireland, and other cultures as well. The fiddle music has a crookedness, a fast rhythm that goes along with step dancing at the same time they do the changes.

I can't remember the names of the tunes my family played. Yet today you can pull up "Gilbert's Duck Dance" and hear traditional Métis fiddle tunes. It's the fiddle music I listen to now and sounds a lot like some of the music I remember hearing in my grandma's kitchen. Métis is a French word that means "mixed," the mixed people of Canada.

After dinner the kitchen was alive with fiddle music, along with banjo and guitar playing and Grandma's feet tapping while she step danced with the music. With our southeastern roots, much of the fiddle music I grew up with was a blend of Indian and hillbilly. Today it's called bluegrass, but in those days it was known as hillbilly, or hill, music.

Sometimes after dinner, instead of music, we watched westerns on television. Since Grandma and Grandpa and Dad and I, and all of the aunties, uncles, and cousins, were all Indians, we kids thought it was funny that the black-and-white movies on television showed Indians sitting on horses at the rise of a hill with their faces painted and living in tipis. All of the Indians we knew drove trucks or cars and lived in houses, like we did.

After the movie ended, that's when Grandpa and Auntie rounded up all the kids and told us what we called real-life Indian stories.

Auntie always told us creation stories, the teaching stories, the traditional ones. I loved the story about how Lenape people are one with nature and that the four winds are our family members, grandparents. The spring warm wind was our grandmother. The stars, grandfathers. The sun and moon, brothers whose job it was to lighten and darken the sky.

Grandpa told us hair-raising stories about things that had happened to him as a young boy, as a man, and while raising seven children with Grandma. The remembering often sent Grandma outside to sit on the back porch. When the storytelling ended, I went out back and sat on the porch with Grandma, and we smelled the rain or watched the stars, one by one, begin to light the sky and let the chill air of mother earth embrace us.

Grandma often reminded me that her Indian ways were mostly Cherokee ways because that's what she had grown up knowing from her mamma, and it was mixed with her daddy's ways from his people in Scotland.

Squinting at me, Grandma said, "Child, your Indian is Cherokee, from me and from your grandpa and your papa, and their Cherokee is mixed with Lenape and Seneca, and you must always remember. Who knows, maybe your Lenape or Seneca people will be the ones to call you home." I was eleven years old. We were sitting out back, shelling beans. Too young to understand the complexities of tribal belonging or what it meant to be mixed Indian, mixed with white, and I tucked her words into my heart for safekeeping, like I did with the things Auntie often said.

I don't have any pictures of my dad's side of the family. The film was overexposed the day we all lined up according to our generation. In the first photograph my grandfather, Auntie, and all the great-aunts and uncles are grouped together. These are my grandfather's siblings; they are mostly mixed Indian, and the line didn't hold a white face. The next group photographed was my dad, his sister, and all of the younger aunties and uncles and all of their cousins. This is the first half- and mixed-blood generation in our family. Some have both parents with Indian blood, and others have one white parent, so depending upon who their mother or father partnered with, this generation had eyes of brown or hazel, wavy or straight dark hair.

My brother and I stood with the largest group of Cherokee, Lenape, and Seneca cousins. We were more mixed than our parents. As we stood together, I remember thinking about how we were not full bloods or even half, and yet we weren't white and never would be, and someday we would become the elders in our family.

With our hillbilly roots mixed with Indian, *slight white* is a term I grew up hearing.

Outsiders couldn't place us. My dad's family wasn't like other white folks, and we weren't like Indians who lived on the reservation.

When I was twelve, my dad's father said to me, "Sometimes it's better not to claim you're Indian."

Understand he had experienced much discrimination. He looked full Indian and grew up with the warnings and the fear in the years after the U.S. Congress passed the Religious Crimes Code. American Indian people were forbidden to hold religious ceremonies or conduct prayer. Indian parents were forbidden to teach children our customs, traditions, and language or share songs and stories. Anyone who did could be put in jail. The law required American Indians be made over in the image of white Americans.

The Religious Crimes Code was passed in 1883, and it wasn't until the passage of the Indian Religious Freedom Act of 1978 that Native peoples were permitted the freedom to live Indian lifeways intrinsic to cultural sovereignty.

The Religious Crimes Code was in effect throughout most of my grandfather's life, and it was in effect throughout my childhood and teen years and into my early adulthood. Auntie had taken a great risk in the 1950s and early 1960s when she told us her stories.

My grandfather wanted to forget. But Auntie and Uncle (Grandpa's younger sister and older brother) wanted to remember. The old ways were important to Uncle, and I longed to know what he knew. I wished he'd take me with him to the stomp dances and to those other secret places he went dressed in beadwork and deerskin leggings. But my grandpa shot angry arrows out of his eyes, so I knew I was not supposed to want it.

In 1971, when I was eighteen, I had my first opportunity to fill out one of those forms that asks you to mark your racial status. In those days it said to check only one box.

My dad was with me.

"What should I do?" I gasped.

I was at the reception counter, filling out the form under bad fluorescent lighting, and there was a long line of people behind me.

"Take your time," my dad said. "This is the most important decision you will ever make."

I chose the box labeled American Indian.

10

UNDOCUMENTED

The year I turned sixty-five, I discovered my grandfather had been enrolled in the Cherokee Nation. My grandfather was practiced at keeping his secrets.

For the record, I am not enrolled, and my father was never enrolled. We are unpapered and undocumented. Why am I not tribally enrolled? This question always comes up, and for most of my life, I didn't know why. I figured it had something to do with Grandma. All her life Grandma had been a Cherokee. She was born in 1888, and in 1953, the same year I was born, when she was already well into her sixties, the government decided her kind of Cherokee blood, which traced back to South Carolina, ought to be Lumbee. Maybe this is just hearsay, I don't know. She died when I was sixteen. If I could go back, I'd have a long talk with her and get her to tell me more. What has stayed with me is how Grandma claimed it was just folks talking and that a piece of paper from the government couldn't change anything. She said her Cherokee people had been divided and scattered into odds and bits, and they were determined to keep their lifeways alive.

Growing up, I accepted not being enrolled as normal for light-skinned mixed Indian people like me, mixed with white and with Black ancestry, scattered and erased.

Late in life I discovered enrollment was a possibility. If I'd had the opportunity when I was young, I would have jumped for it, without giving it a second thought. Enrollment and citizenship would lend credibility, satisfy those who doubted and questioned me. It would come in handy when I was challenged about whether or not I was Indian enough.

But if I had gained enrollment when I was born or decades ago, when I was a teenager, or as a young adult or even in middle age, I would have had many years to learn the life lessons it held and to learn to carry the responsibility enrollment within the Cherokee Nation brings.

Yet claiming it at sixty-five, without having any of the lived experience, felt disrespectful to me and a privilege I had not earned.

When I was young, I held regrets about not being enrolled. It was just one more way of proving I was not good enough. But now I'm at peace with the way my life has unfolded. Now there is something else equally important to me, and I'm glad to have had many years to give it more thought. I'm Cherokee, Lenape, and Seneca, and I cannot tease apart the layers and belong to one tribe more than another. My blood is a mix, merging to form a third—a mixed-blood—and I'm dwelling with utmost respect between the boundaries.

11

GROWING UP

My growing-up years were divided, with time spent with both my father's and my mother's family. With my paternal great-grandparents a central part of our lives, it meant that I grew up with three grandmothers and three grandfathers. It also meant that in my childhood I spent Saturday in the white world and Sunday in Indian Country, always between both worlds.

Since my dad's parents were divorced, I got to know each of them separately. My memories of my dad's mother are not the same as my father's. My grandmother had time for me, and I felt loved. She bought me sharp new crayons and sat on the floor with me, coloring and drawing. I could touch and move around the knickknacks filling her shelves.

She wasn't Indian. She was born to German immigrants on a farm in rural Kansas. Her mother had Jewish heritage that no one ever talked about. Her parents immigrated to the United States many years before World War II.

My grandmother was also a storyteller. When we had tea in the afternoons, folded together in the turquoise vinyl chair, she told me stories about her childhood that sounded like truth braided with fiction because all of her stories had happy endings.

By the time I was old enough to notice, my mother's mother had softened and had lost her angry edge. My maternal grandmother sewed the dresses I wore to school. She let me select the fabrics and colors and was never angry with me. After years of silence, she began sharing stories about her life. She grew up dirt-poor in rural Nebraska, and her family forged food and herbs from the wild. Her birth certificate stated she was born in Indian Territory, but she didn't know where. Although she identified as white, she wondered about the connection her mother had with the Indian women living nearby. Often she was cared for by one of these women. She called her "Auntie," but my grandmother had no idea if Auntie was a blood relative or a close friend of the family.

"When I was a young girl," Grandma said, "I only had two flour sack dresses. Each night I had to wash and iron so that I would have a clean dress to wear the next day."

Secretly, I doubted the importance of this much cleanliness. Surely Grandma must have given in to wearing a rumpled dress once in a while. I knew I would have.

"Didn't you get sick of all that washing?" I asked. That day I must have been about eight years old, and I remember looking down and seeing a grape jelly stain on the front of my white blouse. My fingers moved over it and added dirt streaks.

"Oh, you'd be surprised how important being clean is if you only have two dresses," she said. Grandma had just finished making an orange polka-dot cotton sundress for me, and now she was ironing it. She licked her finger and tapped the hot iron quickly. A sharp hiss of steam exploded around her finger.

When my grandmother was eleven years old, she taught herself to sew and to make her own patterns and discovered she had a special talent with fabric, always managing to get the material fitted together to make a perfect dress.

In my teenage years, in the 1960s, she made dresses and miniskirts for me that were extra short, with just enough material for me to sit down on. Probably shorter than Grandma liked, but she hemmed them just the way I asked her to.

Of all of dresses my grandmother sewed for me while I was growing up, the yellow-and-white gingham and the brown calico with white rickrack around the sleeves were the two dresses I thought of most often. Because when I was a kid, when I imagined what it might be like to be desperately poor, like Grandma was, with only two dresses, in my mind it was these two dresses that I wore every other day, washed, then ironed, each night before I went to bed.

My grandfather played the banjo and mandolin. He was self-taught and had even taught himself to read music. He laughed often and told me stories about his life growing up in rural Colorado, the beautiful land he called home. His family was poor but rich in spirit. He and his twin sister were the oldest of eight children.

We sat at the kitchen table together trading stories, eating black licorice or extra sharp cheddar. He taught me about rodeo life and to feel the way the rhythm of the banjo and the mandolin spoke to me. I felt the tang of each cord and how every song floated in its own color.

When my cousins shouted, "It's too loud—close the door," I sat with my ear tuned to my grandfather's music. While everyone in the family liked hearing him play, I was the only one who liked hearing it all of the time. When he wasn't playing his music, he was growing things in his garden. His backyard was home to me. He often took care of me when I was young.

After we finished in the garden and washed the mud off our hands, my grandfather would rummage through the bookshelves, searching for my favorite story in an old book with yellow pages and a loose binding. He cleared his throat, his reading voice was rough, with an eighth grade education, yet he was a good reader. And when the story ended, he pulled out his banjo and played for me.

My brother was born when I was ten years old, when we were still living in Compton, California. It was 1963, and back in those days, I always went by my full given name, TerryLynn. I was deeply rooted in my mixed-race neighborhood and in the Compton City School District. My best friend was Japanese and Mexican. My friend next door was Bolivian, and her mother loved me like a daughter. On Saturday nights I slept over and drank in the sounds, scents, language, foods, and all things Bolivian.

We lived in a corner of Compton bordering the city of Paramount, with two tiers: white and everyone who wasn't white. I'd walk to the neighborhood meat market, where the butcher sliced twenty-five cents worth of bologna for my brown bag school lunch.

My school PE jersey had *Compton* printed across the front, and when we won the playoff games, we were Compton and we were proud. I had visions of attending Dominguez High School in Compton with my classmates, friendships I'd forged since kindergarten. And just when I had found my rhythm and had everything all figured out—my family moved. The reason for our move was to move up. My mom and dad wanted to lift me out of our extremely diverse, mixed-race, lower-income bracket, high-crime neighborhood.

With the move, the plan was for me to begin assimilating into a whiter working-class neighborhood so I could get in with what my parents thought would be a "better" crowd of kids. Except I had no idea how to do it. You can take the girl out of the neighborhood, but you can't take the neighborhood out of the girl. In my corner of Compton, I fit in, and I knew what was expected of me.

When we moved, my parents urged (pushed) me into making friends with white kids. Except there are different rules and things necessary to know in order to move into a white crowd, and it's not easy being the new girl—from Compton.

When I began attending a new school in South Downey in Los Angeles County, I didn't know how to measure up to white standards. The city of Downey is divided in two. North Downey is the uppity white section, and South Downey, where we lived, is the mixed-race lower end. My high school was a mix of kids from the north and south. My parents had not moved up far enough, and our zip code downgraded us. My skin and eyes were light enough to pass as white, but I had not been raised or groomed to think or behave as a white person, and within white social circles, everything about me was all wrong.

Already I had learned it was better not to let on that I was Cherokee. Anyone with a Cherokee great-grandmother was regarded with suspicion and often even ridiculed. It was commonplace then, and now, to assess those who claimed Cherokee ancestry as not Indian or not Indian enough.

In high school I was not concerned about not being Indian enough. I was still on the brink of discovering that the part of me that carried white blood was not white enough for some white people.

I was beginning to learn that in order to be accepted by certain white people, it mattered who your friends were. When I went to the houses of white kids to hang out after school, I needed to be aware of how I was holding myself at all times. The white mothers always pumped me, asking a series of questions about my family, and if they didn't feel satisfied with my answers, I wouldn't be allowed to stay at their houses for long.

Things would be different when I went over to the houses of my friends of color. Their mothers would always take me in without hesitation. And if there was a grandmother at home who spoke English with an accent or didn't speak English at all, I could usually be certain they wouldn't ask me if my daddy had a job. In their homes I felt safe.

I was also figuring out there were some white people I did not want to become friends with. I learned to stay alert and watch for clues: there might be an older brother who pulled his eyes in an upward slant and said something mean about Chinese people; or a father who casually spouted racial slurs at people of color or made fun of Indians. When this happened, I knew I had to make an excuse to go home, and I'd never go back.

Things began to change for me the year I turned fifteen. I gave up trying to fit in with the elite white kids. I'd lost interest in trying to aspire to the social structure their lives revolved around. The high-status social clubs they joined and the way they worked hard to maintain the standards set seemed pointless to me.

I had begun going out with a mixed-blood boy in my English class. I was drawn to him for our shared common bond. He was raised by his Cherokee mother and had recently moved in with his white father and stepmother. He felt caught between two worlds. We understood each other. Nothing ever needed explaining. It wasn't a romantic relationship, but our friendship continued until he moved out of state, back with his mother. This friendship defined me. It was a marker event in my life, when I knew for certain that white boyfriends and white girlfriends could never know me completely. They would try to understand the core of me that is Indian. I would do my best job of explaining, and something would always get lost in the translation.

It was also the year I felt like I had suddenly stepped from childhood into womanhood. This caused my relationship with my mother to play out in ways that made us more like equals, like girlfriends. But I never knew when she would go into a mother mode and prevail over me. She was barely sixteen years older than me, and I suddenly became aware that she was interested in the same things most of my teenaged girlfriends enjoyed doing. She spent lots of time with me and with my friends. I had the cool mother, and when we went to the beach together, she looked better in a bikini than I did.

Still, I saw my mom as an advantage. She was fun to be with, and having a young mother who was not a typical mom gave me an edge that other girls my age didn't have. Her presence and demeanor made me appear sophisticated. My mother was on a continual quest to find herself, and her search led her to explore existentialism and the counterculture of the 1960s. As a teenager, I was already drawn into this world, and my mother's interest made it possible for it to become a part of my daily life at home.

But proper mothers in working-class neighborhoods like ours were not supposed to wear low-waisted bell-bottom jeans and lace-edged tank tops and smoke marijuana; they were supposed to make a tuna casserole and watch television or knit after dinner. They were expected to have polite, casual conversations with their daughter's friends. Instead, my mother hosted midnight philosophical discussions around the kitchen table, discussing civil rights and Woodstock. She changed her personality just enough to always fit in any crowd. She was what everyone in those days referred to as "hip"—eager to explore; tall, thin, and shapely; with her shag-cut brown hair frosted blonde and head-turning ice-blue eyes.

In contrast, I was short, serious, pretty enough, with an easygoing personality, talkative and friendly, but also too reserved at times, almost to the point of being aloof. A nature-loving, bookish girl, moving through life to my own rhythm. My teen years was an era of hippies, the Jefferson Airplane, and peace signs. Marijuana and free love were commonplace. I smoked marijuana, but I didn't think my mother should. Yet some of my friends had mothers who carried on more than mine did, so I shrugged my worries off. And besides, my mother's best friend, Glenda, a free-spirited Oklahoma-born and -raised mixed-blood, who didn't wear a bra and rode her Appaloosa bareback, made my mother seem conservative.

My father was the opposite of my mother. He was traditional, holding tight to the beliefs commonly held by society at large while retaining his Indian essence. He was also racially aware, could view the world with a person of color lens, and understood what it meant to not have white society privilege. He had frequent conversations with me about race and about how to be street-smart and safe, while my mother, who had grown up with a white identity, was still learning about race. Their unusual mix gave me the advantage to cherry-pick an identity cross-bred with traditional and newly evolving 1960s values.

But my parents' marriage didn't work out. The hostility between them was constant. My father was inflexible and demanding. Things had to be his way. If not, he sulked or got angry and lashed out.

My mother alternated between angry and passive aggressive. She chain-smoked cigarettes late into the night, her hand shaking. She began waking me up late at night, asking me to talk with her so that she could calm down. Quickly, I learned to find the right things to say so that she would relax and I could go back to sleep. I was an anxious girl to begin with, and I found the tension alarming.

Yet all of this made me a good reader. I could pick up a book and travel. Books served as a passport, allowing me to glimpse peoples and terrain unknown to me. I learned to understand and see through the eyes of those who had different lives. Within books I found a multiplicity of lifestyles. Inside, I knew myself to be an artistic free spirit yet without any apparent talent. I could not draw. I showed no promise with arts and crafts. I sang off-key. When I danced, my rhythm was off. In school I was not a high-achieving student, and I had no idea how to study and improve my average grades. My special gift was dreaming and holding faith that whatever it was that I was good at would turn up one day.

12

LUKE

Before my parents divorced, my dad removed himself by working long hours, and often he wasn't around. With one less parent to worry about, I began inviting friends over, and our house became a gathering place. I was sixteen, and at first mostly my girlfriends came over, then I began bringing boys around, and that's when things got complicated and a little bit out of control.

A new pattern developed where it was common for boys who were my friends to drop by and talk with my mom. Other times, boys I didn't know came over to visit with my mom.

Sometimes I'd join in the conversation. But my mother's taste in boy-men was different from mine. I'd stick around long enough to be friendly, then go to my bedroom.

The exception was Luke. He'd arrive at my house unannounced, like the other boys did.

I liked him, and it took me the better part of a year to figure out he came to see me, not my mother.

After I got to know Luke and we became close friends, late at night, when the house grew quiet, we curled up together in an oversized stuffed chair and talked for hours. The cushion sagged, and the sides curved up and folded us tightly together.

Luke's mother stayed drunk most nights, and he had moved his bed into their garage. Often he came to my house. It was 1969. Luke would watch television with me and go home to his garage when *The Tonight Show* ended and Johnny Carson said good night.

The thing I treasured most about my friendship with Luke was how it kept me honest. When I told him something, I knew right away if I was lying to myself, and I could tell that he knew too.

Luke thought I was special—it showed in his eyes—and I liked him more than any other boy. But I didn't like the way he kept me guessing. We weren't dating. It was a friendship where he came to my house, but I never had any idea when he might come over.

Frequently, we spent Friday nights together, but some Fridays he didn't show up, and on Saturday morning he might arrive at my house early, catching me by surprise.

We'd fall into a long day together, lasting late into the night. Then he stayed away for a few days, never calling, and then all of a sudden, he'd drop by again, unannounced.

His unpredictability unnerved me. I resisted a romance with him, refusing attraction or despair, and we became best friends in a minefield of platonic love. To keep my heart locked away from him, I dated others, lots of others. Luke didn't date anyone.

When I was twenty-three, I left Los Angeles and moved to the Central California coast. Luke moved to a small adobe place in New Mexico, backing up to the Rio Grande, near the land his people used for healing. Luke and I stayed close friends. We frequently had hour-long conversations on the telephone, and we exchanged handwritten letters, but we also moved on, into our own separate lives.

13

GARY

I had known Gary from an earlier period in my life. We met in the rough-around-the-edges rural mountain community where my family and his spent time in the summer when we were teenagers. I liked him, and I knew he liked me, but neither of us wanted to be in a long-term relationship, and when the summer ended, we drifted back into our individual lives.

The following summer we did not pick up where we had left off; instead, we began a casual friendship. For the next four years, during the summer, we spent time together within the same crowd of friends at the lake; we went to the same parties at night and stayed friendly.

A few times I invited him and his current girlfriend to dinner at my cabin. Sometimes he would stop by early in the morning for coffee and conversation. At the end of summer, we returned to our city lives, in different cities, miles apart. And then we lost touch.

Over the years we lost contact with each other. Then one day, unexpectedly, our paths crossed. I invited him over. We got along well and began seeing each other every weekend.

Gary lived far enough away that we had to have a long-distance relationship, and we could only see each other when we had weekends off from work. He was outgoing, gregarious, loyal, and tenderhearted. A careful observer, eager to help others, he had boundless energy when he was in a happy mood.

I have an average amount of energy. I'm neither low nor high, and sometimes when he was tired, Gary's energy level matched mine. We made a good team. His mood was constantly changing, while mine was predictable. He provided me with variety, and I provided him with consistency. I was the budget balancer, and he craved abundance, and we both had a thirst for adventure.

After two years the driving distance began to wear us down.

"It might be easier if we could live together," Gary said.

I blinked for a moment, then sidled up next to him and shrugged.

"But we would need to get married first," he said.

"Why?" I asked.

"My parents are traditional, old-school, and I don't want to upset them."

I did not look up. I just stood there.

Gary's parents were conservative, proper, but not elite. His father had immigrated from Northern Ireland. They were white, Protestant, working-class, of comfortable enough yet meager means.

I didn't want to get married. I wanted to live together first and discover what it would be like if we were together on a daily basis. There was some friction in our relationship, and I had doubts. Gary alternated between happy-go-lucky, highly extroverted, and moody. I never knew what mood he would be in when we got together at the end of the week. He enjoyed parties, was well liked by everyone, and he drank heavily at times.

I wanted to take it slow and make sure getting married was the right decision. Also, I was not sure if I wanted to marry a white man. I needed more time to think about it. Still, I had fallen in love with a white man.

Gary felt our conflicts were a result of the strain he was under due to our long-distance relationship and job stress and from dealing with the heavy traffic he faced driving from his house to mine, and he thought that by living in the same household, things would calm down.

The second time Gary brought up the subject of marriage, I said yes.

I married for love, and things never did calm down.

14

LEAPING INTO WOMANHOOD

Early on, I made sure Gary and Luke got along well together. Sometimes we visited Luke, and we three shared a pizza and a six-pack and picked up where we had left off, hanging out as if no amount of time had passed.

Other times I visited Luke alone, or he came to our place. In those days we had frequent casual dinner parties and late nights filled with guitar playing and laughter. Often friends spent the weekend with us, including Luke.

My younger brother, now a teenager, regularly stayed with us too. Sometimes my mother spent the weekend with us, and usually she brought a friend, and often the friend was not much older than I was. When we had large gatherings, my other guests were surprised when they learned that she was my mother. She fit right in and slipped in and out of our lives seamlessly.

With our home so often filled with casual dinner parties and overnight guests, it took me a while to figure out that Gary required more freedom and alone time than I do.

The reticent side of my personality is gentle. I slip into a reserved state softly. Gary could flip from seemingly peaceful and outgoing to reserved and harsh. This change would always sneak up on me. While I require a certain amount of freedom, I'm also like a caged bird, but the cage door must remain open. As long as the door is open, I stay content knowing I can go out when I want. In my mind Gary needed a wide-open field, and he could never be caged. He was a loving husband and, after we had kids, a devoted father, but he was also a slave to moods that caused him to grow distant and pull away from me. Sometimes for days at a time he brewed, and he seldom shared what he was thinking and feeling during these episodes. This bothered me. Or he wanted to go fishing on the ocean for a few days, which didn't bother me at all because either way I was alone.

"You're going to be a fishing widow," other fishermen's wives warned. But I didn't mind. Time apart provided balance and gave me the alone time I craved so that I could continue to be outgoing. I teased Gary, saying his life, love, and second lady was the sea.

After we became parents, we were nearly always at home together with our kids. We took turns cooking dinner; usually, he washed the dishes, and I dried. After he wandered off, leaving the sink full of water, I took the dishcloth and wiped down the table and the counters. We took turns giving the kids baths and reading bedtime stories, and a few times each year, we gave each other the gift of being able to have a weekend to ourselves.

15

THE WAY OF
THIS MOTHER

We waited five years before starting a family. First, I gave birth to our daughter, Vanessa, and discovered I loved being a mother. When our daughter was three, we adopted our son, Jay, when he was one year old. Usually, infertility prompts couples to pursue adoption, but I have never experienced infertility, and when we decided to add more children to our family, we chose adoption. We wanted to make a difference in this life by parenting kids who were already born, waiting, needing a family.

Since I'm Native American, naturally we first looked into an American Indian adoption. The Indian Child Welfare Act of 1978 (ICWA) requires efforts first be made to place American Indian children with birth relatives, then with tribal members. To apply with the Native American Adoption Exchange, adoptive parents need to provide an enrollment number or certificate of degree of Indian blood. But I'm undocumented. I would have been able to secure Native community references stating my belonging and degree of Indian blood. Yet since Gary is white, and I am well aware of the barriers and racism he would face, we decided he was not fully prepared to adopt an Indian baby.

For some American Indian people, white is the face of the enemy, the colonizer, the conqueror. This was a fact I had learned to adjust to at an early age. Being light-skinned, it was something I dealt with on a regular basis. But Gary felt he might not be able to handle the hostility he was likely to experience. Instead, we adopted our son from South Korea, a country that was bursting with orphanages in 1982.

With my strong belief in ICWA, my basic philosophy holds tight: race, culture, and heritage are important, not just for Native American children but for all children. As my son's mother, I believed I was responsible for leading him to people who could teach him something of Korean ways and beliefs. I knew he needed to grow up feeling at home within the Korean American community. This led me to making new friendships with some of the Korean families living near us.

Soon I discovered the element of Korean culture I love best—the tradition of community belonging, with neighborhood families gathering and everybody pitching in to cook, bring food, and help out. I felt like I was at a family reunion. Being within a group in which everyone was 100 percent Korean, with brown-black eyes and very dark hair, took me back to my growing-up family, to my dark-skinned grandparents, aunties, uncles, and the black-haired older cousins I so little resembled.

I'm short, and at least most of the Korean women were as short as I am, and my olive skin, small deep-set eyes, and strong-boned face felt right at home. There was no time to wonder if I would be accepted; many of the Korean women extended their kindness to our family time after time.

Perhaps some in the Korean community oppose Korean adoption, but many people opened their arms to us. Since those who are not Korean do not romanticize Korean culture in the same way some who are not Native tend to romanticize Native American cultures, few Koreans have experienced the attempt by those who are not Korean to assume their culture and claim a heritage that does not rightfully belong to them.

Over the years we formed close, heartfelt friendships and gained Korean American friends who became stand-in grandparents, aunties, uncles, and cousins, and I sunk deep roots into Korean lifeways.

When our daughter was six and our son four, we added a third child to our family, a ten-year-old girl, also of Korean descent. She came to us from foster care and had spent her first ten years in multiple foster homes. She was sad and angry, with unresolved emotional and behavioral problems stemming from abuse, neglect, deprivation, and rejection in her early and middle childhood years. We sought ongoing counseling, but there was some kind of barrier we couldn't break through. Never one to waste money or admit defeat, I spent those therapy sessions discovering my own thorns; we all have them.

What if a social worker had thought to ask her if she wanted to be placed in our family and if she wanted to be adopted?

Eventually, our family therapist did ask her. She said, "No, I didn't want another new family, but nobody listened to me."

Time with this daughter ran through my fingers like sand. She lived with us for seven years. When she was seventeen, she made the decision that she did not want to stay in our family. She moved out and relocated to a different state and drifted out of our lives.

In the few years we had together, I know she tried hard, and I reached deep to find a route into her heart. What I want to remember are the days when our mother-daughter relationship was a slender strip of orange heat filled with promise. Ripe and seductive, like summer love. But it would remain sultry, like an affair that couldn't quite get started.

Those seven years while I worked to form a bond with this child were some of the hardest years of my life. I felt that I should have been able to do better, be a better mother.

After she moved out, without my newfound friendships with Marie, Ann, Mary Lou, and Irene, I might not have survived this loss. By introducing me to the seven ways she lived her life, Marie was helping me begin to move forward, to see beyond my role as a mother, and to look past the boundaries I set for myself as a mixed-blood. Ann steadied me as I began to emerge as a Native woman. With Mary Lou I was learning to trust myself. Irene kept me laughing. All four of these women brought joy back into my life. When I fell into episodes of being too serious, they nudged me toward playful.

After this child left our family, we had more family counseling and began to find a comfortable rhythm. Without her rage and angry outbursts, a newfound calm and tranquility took hold. Our homelife became relaxed, and I began getting to know Vanessa and Jay on a much deeper level.

I'd lost the opportunity to be a mother to one child, and I didn't want to miss out on anything with my remaining two kids. I kept my eyes on Jay, watching him talk on the phone with friends, snuck side-glances while he did his homework and when he sprinted out the door to go to school.

Vanessa had a busy school schedule. She was on the track team and had choir practice. Frequently, she was at rehearsals or track meets, and she had a part-time summer job lined up. My kids had busy social lives with their friends, and when they were home, we hung out together in the kitchen, cooking, laughing, and talking.

Gary began working fewer hours. Before then, he had put in twelve-hour days as an escape. Now he was home in the evenings and on the weekends. Good fishing weather had become so important to him that he studied the clouds and scrutinized the sunsets as well as the dawns.

He gauged the winds and collected tackle boxes, rods, and reels. Sometimes Jay was his fishing companion, but it wasn't long before Gary began making friends with some of the men in the Asian deep-sea fishing community.

Our family life together was now what I always hoped it would be, and I wanted to spend all of my free time with my kids. But I knew it would not be good for them or for me.

My best friends were elders, in the winter of their lives. I had no idea how much time I would have left with them. One more Friday or Saturday might be all I had. The brain tumor Jay had been diagnosed with when he was young was an anaplastic ependymoma, and this type of tumor carried a high risk of recurrence. It could return. I had no idea how much more time I might have with Jay. But each time he had an MRI scan, it came back clear.

My passage through the way of the mother was not a typical motherhood journey, and this portion of my life would continue to change. I would always be a mother, but my son and daughter would not always be children. They would grow up and begin to move into the adult world. I could feel myself begin to transition within the seven ways.

Through motherhood I had learned the discipline of sacrifice: my body, my time, my social life and relationships. Everything had been called upon for the service to my children. This stage of life had pushed me to stretch and use all of my capabilities. Motherhood had made me stronger. I was growing far stronger than I ever could have imagined.

16

LUKE AND NEW MEXICO ON MY MIND

Although we talked on the telephone, it had been two years since I last saw Luke. My son and daughter were now old enough to appreciate the freedom of being away from me on occasion. I began making plans to go to New Mexico.

New Mexico and the land beside the river had begun to shape me, and it was a home I carried within. I was beginning to understand that I wanted to spend time with the landscape as much as I wanted to see Luke. The land served as elder and friend.

Luke was now living in a manner that was traditional to his Native ways. The last time I visited him, I had put the pieces together and figured it out. His door opened to the east, facing the rising sun, and his house smelled of old cured hides. He lived close to his relatives—the plants and animals sharing their home with him. He made rattles, and I saw bundles wrapped in red cloth. I knew he had learned to care for the pipe because he had begun smoking his cigarettes in a respectful way. Luke never talked about any of this, and yet I knew because Auntie's stories had always circled back to one thing—walking to greet our return, about the old ways that are still our ways.

What had changed was that Luke had begun walking a structured, disciplined spiritual journey, and this shaped every aspect of his day-to-day life. Elders were guiding him by word of mouth or example. They were teaching him traditions, ceremonies, song and prayer, passed down from one generation to another without written instruction. I did not know many details of these interactions, but I could see it had begun to inform Luke's social attitudes.

What he was experiencing was never discussed in public and often not talked about in private either because a spiritual path is a private journey.

When I arrived at Luke's, I expected it would be the same as all of the other times I had visited. I thought we'd wake at sunrise, go hiking, watch the sunset, and listen to music in the evening. Or maybe we might go into town to the bookstore or grab dinner at the café, like we often did.

Instead, he announced it would be good for me to spend a few days in silence.

The muscles at the base of my neck tightened. "Why?" I gasped.

Luke smiled at me. Laugh lines danced around his eyes.

"Just agree to do it, and then you'll understand," he said.

I watched him take off his hat; his long hair was flattened in several directions and streaked with gray.

In the fireplace flames leaped up, and shadows began to slope across the wall.

A lone coyote yipped, sharp and high. An answer came, closer this time, and then a wild chorus of wavering howls. Luke's dog settled on her haunches, her ears shifted like antennae, then she lowered herself on the floor, listening. I looked into the flames for a long time. The light from the opening in the skylight window was becoming diffuse and gray. We sat by the fire until the last log of the night burned down and the fire fell to pieces.

"It's going to be cold tonight," Luke said, handing me a sleeping bag.

"Can I borrow a T-shirt?" I asked.

"Over there." He pointed to a stack of folded clothes in a basket.

"Good night." he said and crawled through the low doorway and up the stairs.

I watched his tall, lanky body fade into the dark. He was still thin but had gained a bit of weight, thicker around the waist.

His shirt was big on me. I curled my legs and folded it around my knees. The sleeping bag smelled like sunbaked flannel, woodsmoke and pitch from juniper. It was a scent I knew well—it smelled like Luke. I pulled the sleeping bag up around my chin. Fireflies flew in from a small opening in the skylight and wildly darted around the room, clear white beads of light shimmering, flashing, and glowing in the air. I lay silent and felt their current flowing into me, and the tension in the muscles of my shoulders unwound with each breath I took.

The next morning at sunrise, Luke gathered a few things and said he was going to cross the river, camp, and spend some time alone too. For the rest of the week, I entered a silent world where the thoughts inside my head never sounded louder.

Luke had filled the refrigerator. Good coffee beans and a grinder sat on the kitchen counter, bread and fresh fruit.

On my first morning alone, I sat on the roof porch, drinking coffee, watching the river run, and my mind reeled. Thoughts about my family at home, my job, future and past medical appointments for my son, the school conference ahead, carpools, bills to be paid, endless arrangements, phone calls to be returned, and ideas for freelance writing projects—and thinking about how I had expected the week to be, and here I was, alone.

My day ahead was empty, without anything to do, nothing demanding my time. The wind was warming up for the afternoon, and my thoughts thundered in my head.

I wrote in my journal, with my jaw clenched, emptying my mind onto the pages. Next, I read an entire book. I took a nap. Then I went for a long walk, while more thoughts raced through my mind.

After a dinner of bread and cheese, I sat in the rocker by the open window and watched the evening shadows fold into dim gray light. With a new awareness, both funny and painful, I began to understand I wasn't supposed to be thinking about anything. The purpose of silence was to quiet my mind. But it was impossible for me to not think, not worry, and not plan. I tried to hush my thoughts, and my mind shimmered on the edges of sanity.

That night I slept in Luke's bed upstairs and drifted with the ebb and flow of my wild mind until I fell asleep. The next morning the sun was bright in a cloudless sky. Moments after I woke up, my mind went wild again, and I was irritated.

Spending time alone, thinking about whatever I wanted, daydreaming and allowing my mind to romp in a wild field of thoughts, tempted me. But my overactive mind was out of control. I needed to figure out how to put my thoughts to rest.

My simplified living conditions helped clear my mind. I didn't have a closet full of clothes, only a small backpack. Less worry about what to wear. I was living in a small adobe cottage without a car, and there wasn't any place I needed to go. No telephone needing to be answered and no computer. A two-burner stove and plenty of food. I didn't have to do necessary cleaning. No curtains, the trees gave privacy. When I was inside, I kept the door open, and bird sounds drifted in. Or I drifted out for a walk.

Simplification of my outward life continued to slow down my thoughts. I could pick simplicity over complication. Seeing how little I needed to get by and feeling happier than usual gave me extraordinary freedom and peace, and I began to shed my anxiety about many things.

To still my thoughts, I focused on the wind blowing on my face, the way the sun cast light through the trees, and the scent of pinion. I studied a cricket strolling along the floor and the beams in the ceiling veiled with cobwebs. I watched them bend and sway in the wind, and when my thoughts ran away, I pulled them back into the moment.

Each morning I sat by the river.

Live water heals memories. The river spilled toward me, streaming, and I felt my spirit fill. I imagined myself as a river rock, tumbling in the raging water, with my rough edges and hard spots rounded, softened, and my mind let go of deadlines and schedules.

While sitting on a large boulder by the river, a large lizard crawled up the pant leg on my jeans. I sat motionless. We spent a long time together, the lizard on my lap and me, and no agenda other than sunning ourselves, until she crawled away. Auntie always said lizards are a good omen, to be smiled on, and they came to help us learn to be more optimistic and adaptable.

At night I watched the moon rise full and wide in the corner of the sky. It was subtle, but I felt the change; the air was turning from late summer to early fall. After I figured out how to turn down the volume on my thoughts, my dreams became abundant. I found the trapdoor in my mind where, upon opening it, the past and the future were one.

Each morning I pulled my long brown hair into a braid, and on day four, when I looked into the mirror, my face looked relaxed. The lines at the corners of my eyes had softened.

The next day Luke came home at sunset. I was sitting near the door, and I watched him come into view in a yellow-orange light pooling between the trees. He dropped his gear on the porch and sat down next to me. We talked a bit, but mostly we were quiet together. Time slipped slowly. The wind came up. Twilight gave way to darkness.

The next morning we drank coffee and watched the sun rise. We talked for a while and then fell silent and watched the sun climb to the middle of the sky and cover with high gray clouds, and I felt connected. A deep, powerful connection to the earth, sky, wind, connected to me, and to Luke. Before, I had always thought conversation was key for connecting. Now I felt the healing power of silence and how it restored balance.

We eased our way back into the demands of all the necessary things needing to be done until midday. Then I stuffed my clothes into my backpack, and Luke drove me to the airport.

17

AFTER THE FIRST
SILENT WEEK

After that first silent week I spent in New Mexico, everything Auntie had been telling me years before began to take root. The more I began to grasp, the more I understood there was a whole lot more I would never be able to figure out as I walked the seven ways, and understanding came easier when I didn't try too hard. By now I'd figured out it was important to pay closer attention to everyone in my life. They all had something of value to offer, and if I didn't listen, a chance to learn something new might be missed.

While Luke learned from the elders, dedicating himself to a life-style of gaining knowledge of his traditional ways, sometimes I went home for the weekend, and usually my mother's friend Glenda was around. I sat in the kitchen, eating Glenda's frybread, laughing at her stories, with my kids piling the bread with powdered sugar and dropping crumbs on the floor.

Glenda could sew almost as well as my grandmother. She made tiny bikini bathing suits for me with matching cover-ups, and she taught me how to fringe the sky-blue shawl my daughter would later dance in. Over the years we had developed a pattern of frequently trading things and borrowing back and forth. I gave her the purple suede fringed bag, gifted to me, that I didn't feel comfortable carrying, and she gave me the handmade ribbon shirt, Indian Plains style, gifted to her, that was too traditional for her taste. She favored trendy clothes, and her wardrobe was peppered with the latest styles.

On this day Glenda was wearing a new pair of beaded earrings.

"Nice earrings," I said. There was a heartbreaking quality of lightness in the way the strands of turquoise beads reflected light.

"Be careful." She slid her glasses down her nose and winked at me.

"If I followed the traditional way, I'd have to give these to you. The elders say that when a younger woman admires something, you must be generous and give it to them."

I flopped back on the couch. "But what if someone admires something and you don't want to give it up?" I asked.

She smiled. "There's a way to get out of it. You say my grandmother gave it to me, and it's the only thing I have of hers. It shows you are respectful, and it won't offend anyone if you say it like that."

Glenda was ten years older than I was, and she understood me in the way that only another mixed-blood can. When I was young, I wanted to be like her: daring, mischievous, with a ready laugh and those dark chocolate-melting eyes.

Later that night we built a fire, and with my feet propped up on the hearth, gazing into the dancing flames, Auntie showed up, just as fierce in my mind as she had been in life. I felt our lives intertwine, and I remembered the way she answered my questions by telling me to put it in my holy center and not to think about it too much, to just let the answer come in its own time. I was returned to the times when Auntie would surprise me by talking about what was good medicine and bad and how to figure out what to do, and not do, if power was given.

Auntie's shoulders had bent as she grew older, but she always stood straight as a young girl when she told me her stories.

18

JUST WRITING

Marie began her day early, doing the yard chores first. She invited me to stop by any time, but it had to be before eight. By nine she would be at her writing desk.

When I arrived, she was on her way out the door with a bucket in each hand. She handed me a bucket. Every berry bush in her yard was a mass of white blossoms, green berries, pink and ruby berries. It took us an hour to get through the patch.

Marie set down her bucket of berries and turned toward me. Her eyes black and deep. She stared straight at me, stopping two rows away.

"You are a hard worker, and you are good at giving."

I shrugged.

We stared at each other for a moment.

Marie gave me another long look. "But you don't know how to receive."

I stepped back and slumped my shoulders.

Marie laughed and walked over to where I was standing and wrapped her arm around my waist. "And you are too serious. What do you like to do for fun?" she asked.

I did not reply.

She looked up at me. "What do you enjoy?"

"Reading."

"What else?"

I shrugged. "Reading and writing."

I looked up to catch her eye.

She was quiet for a while, and together we listened to the sound of a car passing by.

I crossed my arms and hunched my shoulders tight. "But I have a feature article due next week, and my work is drying up just when it was going so well," I burst out.

Marie leaned in toward me. Our breath floated between us in the early-morning air. "What else have you been doing for fun, other than writing?" Marie asked.

"Nothing else."

"If your life is too thin, your writing won't be full," Marie said. We stood together like two trees that had grown on the path overnight, and she was the taller one.

"It has always been my feeling that writing must come out of living," Marie said in her clean voice. "Go somewhere. Do something to help someone, and don't write."

Her advice sent an energy that tickled the back of my neck.

"And have some fun." She laughed again and pointed at a patch of Mexican sage. "Bright-red flowers scatter over it in the fall." She cupped the sage in her hands. "Oh, well, goodness," she said, gathering up a large clump. "It's getting leggy. I need to cut it back. Usually, I put the pruning tips in water on a table in the house. Makes a nice nosegay. Want to take some home?"

I gathered up the sage cuttings and went home and called Irene.

"I'm dancing at a powwow on Saturday, and I need a ride," she said.

When I honked my horn on Saturday morning, Irene stepped out of her vintage 1950s trailer house wearing a red windbreaker and a black baseball cap, with *Native Pride* embroidered in bold red letters across the front.

She tossed a duffel bag filled with her dance regalia in the back and climbed into the passenger seat. I rolled down my window and leaned over to help her buckle her seat belt, and we were off.

"How come it's so hot in here?" she asked.

"The heater won't turn off," I said.

Irene rolled down her window as fast as she could. Then she pulled off her hat and began fanning herself.

"It's official," she said, "you're driving an Indian car now."

"Indian car" is a Native joke, meaning something annoying, or lots of things, is wrong with your car—like in the movie *Smoke Signals*, when the car drove only in reverse.

At the powwow I left my thoughts behind. Everything felt slow and relaxed, and nobody was in a hurry. The wind whipped and flapped anything that wasn't tied down.

Irene was not following the seven ways. I thought of her as walking her own path: the way of fun. When I watched her get ready to dance the competitions, I could see a glint in her eye, like a young girl who just couldn't resist the lure of powwow nightlife and maybe catching an Indian cowboy.

We congregated with everyone at the run-down little frybread stand where you could get the best tacos. The dust and wind and the sun mingling with the smells were wonderful.

At the dinner break, picnic tables were stacked with metal pans and pots of hot food for the dancers. The meal was offered as a giveaway, an honoring for one of the dancers. All elders, dancers, and their families were invited to take part.

Irene got in the dinner line, and I asked one of the women serving up the food if I could help. I was in luck. They did need more helpers. I was given the job of dishing out heaping bowls of spicy buffalo chili, offering a bowl to each person in line. There was chatter and laughter all around me, and I had a few moments of conversation with each person wanting chili. If someone wanted grated cheese or hot sauce to go with it, I offered that to them too, and our conversations grew deeper. Some told me five-minute stories, and I felt connected to their lives. The person standing next to me, serving, topped the chili off with a big slab of cornbread. I listened to the happy sounds of voices mixed with our outdoor kitchen clatter. Helping out was some of the best fun I've ever had.

I wanted to do more community volunteering, and helping to serve dinner at the powwow was as good as a place as any to start. By the end of the evening, I knew it was the best place to start. Everyone passing through the dinner line said kind words of thanks to me, more thanks than I deserved. I felt like I ought to be thanking them for providing me with so much joy while I scooped out bowls of chili.

When we had finished serving the guests, we servers took turns dishing out bowls of chili for each other, piling it with cornbread.

After we cleaned up, I joined Irene in the arena for the intertribal dances. I felt the heartbeat of the drum. All around us Indian people were dancing, wearing soft moccasins.

Men and women were carrying babies while they danced. Boys and girls were fancy dancing, and the elders and the old, old ones who barely moved stayed close to the earth.

The sun set through the gathering twilight, and we danced until a full moon rose.

19

WINTER OF HOPE

More often, I remembered Marie's advice not to allow my life to become too thin. My son had bounced back from cancer and a brain tumor, and my cousin Victor, who had AIDS, was going through a stretch of time when he felt less sick. He wasn't healthy like I usually felt; his good health was more like when I had a bad case of the flu.

I decided to spend the weekend with my cousin and his longtime partner, John.

John said it helped greatly when friends came by. Then he was free to spend the day alone in his studio and work on his art. Being helpful was a bonus, but I would have wanted to be there even if I wasn't helping. I adored Victor and John; we always had fun together.

When I slept over, my bed was a wide window seat with a thick mattress and white linen sheets and a white down comforter lightly scented in bleach. In the winter my view overlooked a forest of pine trees covered with snow. After Victor got sick, usually he slept in this bed, and while I was there, he struggled up the stairs to sleep in the master bedroom loft, with John.

Sometimes we cooked dinner together. Cooking together meant Victor washed the shrimp, deveined them, chopped the Swiss chard, got the water boiling for pasta, then ran out of energy and from a rocking chair told me how to assemble the rest of the meal.

Victor had full-blown AIDS. It was back in the days before AIDS meds were available. Already he had lived many years longer than doctors had predicted. Of course, I knew my cousin was going to die. He was comfortable talking about dying, but he was also busy living.

At four o'clock in the morning, when both of us couldn't sleep, Victor served me coffee in bed. We lit dozens of white candles and talked until the sun came up, and we let ourselves feel something that felt like spirits leave the room. Still, I was like a little girl, not really believing his death would happen.

The next day a friend of Victor's rented a dog sled complete with a guide to take us mushing. Victor, wearing two sets of long underwear under his clothes, rode in the canvas-covered basket, while I balanced my feet on the narrow sled in the front with the driver.

The following morning we spent an hour together at the hospital, while Victor went through a decontamination procedure, but this was ordinary stuff for my cousin.

He joked, "I've given up flossing my teeth to make room in my schedule for more doctor's appointments." Not flossing teeth because they would not be needed for much longer was almost impossible for me to grasp.

Then came the day when Victor grabbed me by the arm and pulled me close.

"I have an appointment to meet with a mortician. I'd like you to come with me."

I tensed and tightened my toes. "Yeah, I want to go with you," I said.

"Are you sure? It'll be pretty emotional."

"Yeah," I said again. "I want to go." The snow tires clicked over the road. I glanced out the window; we were surrounded by snow-covered pine trees shimmering in the sunlight. The roads were icy. By the time we arrived at the mortuary, faint lines of silver shone through a darkening sky.

We stamped snow from our boots, and my cousin opened the door. The room smelled of lilacs. I timidly peered around the corner;

the mortician, dressed in jeans and a blue flannel shirt, came out to greet us.

"Sorry about my appearance," he offered. "I don't usually dress so casual."

"I'm glad you're not wearing a suit," I told him. I was developing laryngitis, and my throat ached.

"We spoke on the phone yesterday," Victor said, and then he added, "I'm looking for a pine coffin." I stared at my cousin, thirty-eight years old and struggling to stand up. I thought about us together earlier that morning, sitting on the couch, my feet in his lap, both of us laughing.

We were led down a narrow hall to a large room filled with coffins. There were metal coffins made of copper, bronze, a choice of leather or velvet interior.

"This looks like an automobile showroom on the moon," I blurted out. "I wouldn't be caught—"

"—dead in one of these." Victor finished my sentence for me and laughed. "That's why it's important to pick out your own." His laughter helped me relax.

A pine coffin sat near the back of the room, almost out of sight. Slowly, gently, I ran my fingers across the wood, a choke swelled in my throat. Tears began to sting, and I willed them to stay in my eyes. My cousin pulled me close and put his arm around me; our eyes met. I took a deep breath and let the tears roll off my chin.

A month later Victor lost his balance coming down the stairs. He fell on top of his eleven-foot-tall, carefully decorated Christmas tree. Our eyes met. I helped him up. This time we couldn't laugh or even cry.

When I was at Victor's house, we shared the same tiny bathroom; we used separate towels for drying our hands. While lying awake for most of a night in my cousin's bed with white moonlight across my face, I got scared and panicky. Although it was the early years of the AIDS epidemic, it had already been medically proven impossible to contract AIDS just by having casual contact with someone infected with the virus; still, buried in my heart was the secret fear of somehow bringing the HIV virus home with me. My son was a cancer survivor. What if I somehow managed to give AIDS germs to my son?

That night I got up at least fifteen times to go to the bathroom; nerves ripped through my stomach. The small sound of an owl pushed against the night. I wanted to be fearless, but even with all of my great medically backed knowledge, I had to settle for being brave.

20

THE RED RIBBON BRIDGE

When I was hired at American Indian Health as a program director, I thumbed through the stacks of program paperwork, thinking about my cousin Victor. The goal of this urban American Indian project was to provide spiritual and cultural connection to Native Americans living with AIDS and HIV disease by incorporating Indian doctoring and traditional values. This was before HIV meds, back when there was little hope for patients with AIDS.

"I'm not that bad yet," Victor often told me. But he had full-blown AIDS and was sick all of the time, and yet he soldiered on. Victor had grown up living a rural life in the California desert. He knew about the wind being different colors from the north and the south and could find footprints in the hills, feel the sound of a hawk out of sight. I remembered how when we were young, we could fly in our minds to faraway places while our bodies climbed through sagebrush and red ants.

Before my cousin got sick, he hosted big dinner parties for his friends at his house with firelight dancing off the one hundred–year–old glass door he used as a dining table.

"Tell me again how you make batter-fried squash blossoms?" I asked every summer. Then came the day when I asked my cousin that question for the last time. A week later he died.

The first day I began working at American Indian Health, I learned that six directors had quit within a span of four years. The task of administering the last year of the Red Ribbon Bridge five-year grant program fell to me. And my to-do list was long because the coordinator position had been vacant for six months before I came along, and I had a lot to learn.

My boss and my coworkers were my own Native people, but I felt like an observer, outside looking in, because as a mixed-blood, in order to belong, I had to prove myself. Prove I was Indian enough.

The Native grant I was hired to administer read like a map, charting the direction of the project. The first thing I did was make phone calls to the handful of people who had last participated and discovered every one of them felt the Native cultural linkages they'd lost since taking part in the program were equal to the health they'd lost. Within each story there was common ground, that with spirituality, community, and hope, they would be able to become the person Creator intended them to be.

Still, most of those I spoke with claimed that after being diagnosed with AIDS and spending tremendous amounts of time being treated by white doctors, living as a Native American person in a predominantly white medical environment made them feel isolated. My job was to help them navigate the medical world while still allowing their cultural ways to be a natural state of being.

I can't remember a time when my core Native values did not define my life. Still, it takes very little to rock my confidence. I felt intimidated and wasn't sure if I knew enough. To make sure I didn't muddle things up, I hired a cultural liaison to work with me, a man who was well respected and established in our Native community.

Ann was coordinating a different program, and we were getting along rather well, sharing the office space together. Gray, the cultural liaison I hired, joined us in the small space. We brought in another folding chair, took turns with the computer, shared the desk, and luckily, we three got along well together.

I liked Gray. We made a good team; we had similar values and the same goals for the project. We could argue, change our minds, and think of solutions to our multitude of challenges. That's when I discovered I understand plenty more than I give myself credit for knowing.

I became even more sold on the idea of what the program could accomplish after reading through the reports of the first four years. But I was the seventh project coordinator hired in a span of four years, and there had been nearly as many cultural liaisons involved who had left the project as well.

Why, I wondered, had so many Native people given up on what seemed to be an ideal employment environment with an opportunity to help Indian people with AIDS connect with core values and connections they felt were missing in their lives?

Although the grant gave specific guidelines of what needed to happen and be documented on paper in order to receive funding, the controls were lenient enough to maintain a strong Native identity, on Indian terms. The purpose of what the last year of the project could be came into focus.

Then immediately, I hit a barrier. Was it my imagination, or did our Native American CEO conceive her staff of Indigenous people like Lewis and Clark had? Like we were dependent wards, expected to be good little Indians and not ask too many questions. Frequently, excellent staff members were severely reprimanded for minor incidents, and I made a mental note to be very, very good, and this was my first mistake.

We often hear the question, is the glass half-full or half-empty? From the sky the lights of our little American Indian community center appeared to glow as one lamp, sending the message that life there was a shared journey, and it was. But I'd met a group of people who were clutching half-empty glasses. Surviving a difficult work situation can be tough, if not impossible, to do alone. I relied heavily on the friendships I made with my coworkers. The conflict we worked under gave us a sturdy bond as our workaday lives intertwined. We were ignoring serious contemporary cultural issues handed down by our Native-run administration, and complaining about it became the glue binding employees together.

That was the worst part; we were afraid to take change by the horns, so we found a way to make our problems seem funny. The laughter saved me, and it also kept me sick. Usually, I'm positive and optimistic, but negativity began to dominate my moods.

The majority of us were each hired to administer a grant for a specific amount of time, and when the grant ended, we would be terminated. We spoke privately, agreeing we would do our very best work, to improve what we could, and when our grant ended, we would leave our worries about the center behind us. But often we stood in the parking lot at the end of the day talking, and the sadness of our situation welled up in us.

At the end of seven months, Gray left the project. Then another teammate gave notice. I wanted to leave too, but I had developed a tolerance for unpleasant situations, so when things didn't seem quite right, I knew how to ignore the feeling and shrug it off. My stomach churned. Soon it brought me to a place where I felt so empty, I became part of the problem—I joined into the complaining, got sucked into the gossip, guzzled it like beer, laughed, and let my mind go numb.

It taught me about something I had not known before—those harmful behaviors people sometimes do to each other collectively as part of an oppressed group have a name; it's called "lateral violence," and it means repeating the repression handed down to us by oppressing our own people.

Then I saw a painting at a community Native arts show, of a woman walking through tall grass with arrows flying at her back. The caption read, "It's good to know my people are behind me." As oppressed people, I began to understand some of us have accepted the values of the colonizer as our own and have handed them down to the younger generation.

I got to thinking about how we had wiped out smallpox and reduced infant mortality, but at my community center, we had replaced it with a far worse epidemic—a sense of distrust and suspicion of our own people. It is the worst of fates to be oppressed by your own sisters and brothers.

Still, the project did manage to help quite a few Native people face end-of-life issues with dignity and keep traditional values. What I learned is the importance of focusing on Indigenous brilliance and success and to make sure younger generations are taught our Indigenous strengths and not to let our Indigenous suffering and trauma override our strengths.

When the program ended, I left the center. Ann left a few months later. And by the end of the year, nearly all of those I worked with had also left. Yet I have become close friends with many of my previous coworkers. We've grown together and learned from our experience.

Over the years our lives are connected in our community as we walk the same sidewalks, bring food when there's a death, and watch each other's children grow up. We don't know how to solve all of our community problems, but at least I've learned not to make fun of a bad situation without doing something to improve it, and as a community, we are growing stronger.

The connectedness we have to each other is so much a part of our lives; it can't be distinguished from our lives. It's in the emails we send each other and the phone messages we leave. At powwows we camp together. Sage from a neighboring tent braids a pungent hint of warmth through the night air. I fill my lungs with it, knowing it will permeate my body and cling to my soul as a reminder of what I can feel when we are all together.

Today a new administration has made the infrastructure at the Indian Health Center strong, and it is thriving. Over the years I've met many Native people in our community who have at one time or another worked for the center. Every one of them is strong, accomplished, doing meaningful and important things with their lives.

Ann said the elders tell us that things happen for a reason. If I had left the center when I first began to question it, I would probably be saying it didn't work. But by plunging in, my disillusionment gave way to a deeper understanding of how all of us pulling together can build a caring, compassionate connection to each other and gain greater strength.

21

THE WINTER THE
STARS FELL

When I read the email saying Luke was dead, I lost my breath, and as I gasped and trembled, I could not swallow to take in more air. I read the words again, closed the email, and reopened it, searching for something, anything, to tell me the message was a mistake.

It had been a while since I last talked with Luke. Yet this was our pattern. A month or two would pass, and then one of us would call. We always picked up right where we left off.

But the last time we talked on the phone, our conversation felt odd, like we were out of step, our rhythm was off. He was grouchy for some reason. I cried; we argued. Then we both stayed on the phone, silent, breathing. We could not bring ourselves together that day. Our disagreements were not unusual. Yet this time it was different. In the middle of it, I cut us off; I said goodbye and hung up.

After a long stretch of time passed without any word from Luke, I called and got a recorded message telling me the number had been disconnected. I sent an email and did not receive a response.

Years ago he had Sun Danced. I wondered if he was dancing again. When he prepared to dance, it was usual for him to withdraw for long periods of time in order to be ready spiritually.

I allowed more time to pass, thinking he'd call me when he was ready to talk.

But I began to feel a void beyond anything that made sense to me. And then came the dreams. A series of dreams with Luke, sweet, deep, and alert. I felt him all around me, peaceful dreams that lingered after I woke up.

I wanted to get into my car and drive straight to Luke's place in New Mexico. Instead, I sent an email to a close friend of his in a nearby town. She owned a business, which made it easy to locate her. I'd met her once, a few years earlier.

She replied immediately, sending me an email saying Luke had died and that a memorial was held at his home by the river, with a large circle of friends and family honoring his walk.

I felt the boundary of time collapse around me. The air smelled different. I tried to swallow past the lump in my throat. The ache in my chest felt hollow, as if it was about to cave in, like I was a candle melting in on myself. Everything felt unfamiliar, new. I was free-falling without gravity pulling me down.

Tears began to roll, slowly at first, and then I was heaving sobs.

Then the phone rang; it was my daughter, calling from school to let me know she had choir practice and would be home late. She suggested I pull the Pendleton blanket off the back of the rocking chair and wrap myself in memories, reminding me that I had been with Luke the day I bought it. That's when I realized it was raining hard, the house was cold, and I was shivering.

With the wool blanket wound tight around me, I thought about the last time I saw Luke. We stood hugging in the middle of the street at the airport, stopping traffic.

Usually, when he drove me to the airport, I'd jump out of the truck, he'd pull my backpack out, and we'd hug fast. Then he would get back into his truck and drive away before the horns began to honk.

But the last time, he leaped out of the truck and grabbed me just as I was about to walk away, he pulled me close, and we hugged and hugged and hugged.

After all, he was the person who taught me to hug and how to hug back in a great big embrace. But first he had to learn how to do it himself.

We both grew up in families that never hugged. Hugging was awkward. I was stiff and barely reached out when someone hugged me, and I made sure to keep a wide space between us. Luke did not hug at all, ever.

Then, one year after he moved to New Mexico, I visited him, and he announced he wanted us to start hugging when we said hello and to hug again when it was time to part. He explained that since neither of us had been hugged as kids and had not been taught to hug, it didn't come naturally to us. But now he had lots of new friends who had grown up hugging, and life with hugging was far better.

So, we started hugging. Stiff at first, but over the years we learned to relax our bodies. We gave short hugs and held tight for the briefest moment and melted into each other. It was the summer I began hugging my friends back when they reached out to me, and I began initiating hugs. I turned into a ready hugger on a regular basis.

Luke was also my memory bank. He could remember things from my growing-up years that I couldn't recall. After we established our relationship as "just friends," he practically lived at my house. With Luke I'd gained an older brother, and it was fun having him around.

When I was growing up, if you came around my house only at suppertime, you would hear folk music, guitar playing, or hard rock. Our kitchen was a place of welcome, with tacos and refried beans fixing to be served, conversation and laughter. If you came around only in the early evening, you wouldn't know about the screaming and yelling, the door slamming, the crying, the name-calling, the pushing and shoving and hitting.

I had blocked it out, but Luke remembered how my dad could turn on my mom and turn a good time into late-night terror. We would creep out of the house, go out back, and sit on top of the narrow cinder block wall, in the dark.

Eventually, the fighting didn't wait for the night; it could happen anytime, and I got better at forgetting.

Years later, after Luke moved to New Mexico, we sat outside on his roof patio watching the river, and he fed memories to me, slowly, gently. I felt safe, and it all came back to me.

The rain pounded the roof, and my tears came almost as fast. I sat thinking about the day at the lake with Luke when I was twenty-two. My brown bikini and my suntanned brown skin. Luke's eyes skimming my stomach, his hands never touching me. And that minefield of platonic love we wandered in.

Once, when we were in our early forties, we talked about how it might have been if we had tried to be a couple. Luke smiled, and I wanted the moment to last forever. Then we both began coming up with reasons why it probably would not have worked out. About how we could never have remained close if we had attempted any type of relationship other than the one we had. Our preferred living styles were too different, and neither of us wanted to change, and we didn't want to change each other or make demands.

We talked about how we might have killed each other with our words. We admitted to being afraid of losing what we had and maintained we needed distance in order to remain close.

Except I know this is just the story we told ourselves. What it came down to was vulnerability—my vulnerability. What I remember about our second year together, when I was seventeen, is that I was starting to care about him a lot, and then I numbed out. After that we turned into friends.

A few years before he died, Luke told me the story the way he remembered it. About how close we had become and how much he loved me when he was nineteen and how remote I became. How hurt he was.

"But I loved you then," I said. "And I still love you."

"I know you did, and I still love you."

We both cried.

"Maybe sometimes people love each other, but it doesn't mean they are meant to be together as partners," Luke said.

We never talked about it again and continued on as we always had, as friends, as if the conversation never happened. And yet from there our relationship began to grow in a new direction. We had changed our friendship by letting go of the nostalgia of the past. We couldn't have gone back to the way we once were even if we had wanted to. Yet in our present way of accepting it as it was, we continued to move in a similar rhythm of intimacy, with hard spots and soft spots, and most of the time it had an easy, unforced feel.

Luke was able to stay open and feel vulnerable and be genuine and kind even in the middle of our most challenging conversations, and it had an opening effect on me.

My husband avoided his own emotions and steered clear of mine. He was loving and caring but quick to anger when pressed into emotional territory. Many years later he made an effort to change. But the years with him while he was shut down made it easy for me to dodge and avoid my own feelings. After decades of either blocking out or glossing over what I really felt, it was difficult learning how to turn my feelings back on.

I liked the way my friendship with Luke pushed me to be open and genuine. I was learning to sit with uncomfortable feelings and allow them to exist without blocking them out or compartmentalizing. But there were still times when I curled up emotionally and crawled within myself, and that is what I did in the last conversation I shared with Luke.

My memories washed over me like a series of massive waves hitting hard, without warning. As soon as I caught my breath, another memory pounded me and pulled me back to 1972, when I was nineteen and got pregnant after a short-lived relationship. Luke was away at school that year, and I was deep inside my own well. Suddenly, I remembered the phone conversation we had when I told him. How calm and steady his voice was, like strong arms holding me across the miles. At the time I didn't tell anyone else that I was pregnant, and without medical insurance, I had to go to social welfare. I sat in the waiting room alone for hours. My shorts were soaked with sweat, and my bare legs stuck to the orange plastic chair. The room was filled with women and crying babies. I thought of my mother at age fifteen, pregnant with me.

"Are you giving the baby up for adoption?" the social worker asked. The question unnerved me. She eyeballed me and hissed, "You've written down that you're American Indian—if it was going to be a white baby, it would be easier to find a family to adopt it."

I clenched my jaw to stay calm. Most strangers didn't place me as Native American. But it would be different for the baby I hadn't meant to create. The father of my child-to-be was a full-blood. In the end I miscarried. A part of me was glad. At least I did not have to make a decision whether or not to surrender my child to another. Yet the pregnancy changed me and sent me in a wholly Native direction. I thought about how often people assumed I was white and about all the white privilege assigned to me. I thought about my dark-skinned cousins who were never assumed to be white. My pregnancy took place in 1972, and I thought about how different the situation would have been if it had happened after the Indian Child Welfare Act of 1978 (ICWA). The law left me able to give birth to a child who would fall under ICWA jurisdiction, and yet without enrollment, I was not Indian enough to adopt an American Indian child.

The baby I was carrying would have grown up to be identified as Native, as American Indian, and would never receive white privilege. I straddled between two races and two groups of people who are more different than alike and who, historically, ethnically, and culturally, do not think the same way or share the same beliefs and value system.

At eighteen, when I made the decision to identify as American Indian, I did not fully comprehend how it would change the course of my life. That day in the social welfare office, I felt the weight I was carrying. It would never be possible for me to live an authentic life with values that were in opposition, and I would always side with Native.

I wondered when Luke first began to gravitate to a wholly Native direction. We never talked about it. Even after he moved to New Mexico and I could see he had taken up his traditional ways, we never had a conversation about it. We were moving in a parallel direction, yet I had no idea when the paths we were following turned onto the same road.

My mind continued to float back over the years. With a new awareness, more memories rolled in and were spread out before me, and I had an aerial view.

I remembered how for two years after the pregnancy ended, I spent long hours working two jobs and maintained a heavy social schedule. Luke was still away at school, and I became reacquainted with Gary.

We had known each other for many years as casual friends when we were teenagers, and then we lost touch. When our paths crossed again, our relationship turned into a swift romance. Long-ago memories, almost forgotten, began to spill out and stuck to me like lint on a black dress. Feelings I'd blocked out began to surface—feelings that had remained untouched in my heart, in that place of perpetual remembering. Validity need have no relation to time, to duration. Uncomfortable feelings I'd felt a long time ago, but would not claim, had taken up root and burst forth, filling me.

I let the twisting ropes untie in my mind. And then I remembered the time Luke was driving, and I sat in the middle, and my brother was in the passenger seat. It had been years since all three of us had been together. We were reminiscing, laughing, and then the talk moved over to mutual memories all three of us shared but had never before discussed.

"Did you sleep with my mother?" I asked Luke.

I knew the answer, but I needed to hear him say it.

"No," Luke said.

I could tell it cut deep that I needed to ask.

Long ago my dad told me he thought they had slept together. I knew that some of the young men who came around our house had slept with my mom. But most of the time, my mom did not have casual flings. She would be with one person for a while, sometimes for months, and then the relationship ended, for whatever reason.

I did not let my dad know what he said about Luke mattered to me, but I was devastated he would believe that Luke, who was my best friend, had slept with my mother. My dad had no idea how much he hurt me by saying it. Fathers and daughters are not supposed to have those kinds of conversations. I never said anything to my dad about whom I thought he slept with.

What my dad said, all those years ago, caused me to have a heavy, sad, feeling I'd been holding in. Suddenly, I felt the full weight of carrying it, how it held me hostage. The release I felt after asking Luke and getting it out in the open made me wish I'd talked with him about it years earlier.

Luke pulled his truck off to the side of the road, killed the motor, and looked at me in a gentle way. He looked into my eyes, and again he said, "No, I did not sleep with your mother."

I wanted to look away, to make that vulnerable feeling disappear, but I held it, and I looked into his eyes, while my brother sat next to me, breathing deeply.

As I sat, remembering, the ache in my throat ran deep into my chest. I wanted to know the circumstances of Luke's death, but I didn't want to contact his friend again. For whatever reason she had not shared details with me, and I didn't want to press. I had waited months before trying to find out what happened to Luke, and whatever it was happened when I was not around. What mattered most was that he was no longer alive. I would never hug him again, never look into his eyes or hear his voice call my name.

Luke was generous, protective, and kind. He brought love and joy into my life, and his death could never take that away from me. We met when I was young and not ready to fall in love. As much as I wished we'd met when I was older and more mature, I wouldn't be the person I am today if I had not had him in my life as a friend for all those years. He taught me what safe feels like.

22

WORDS FACING WEST

After Luke died, I began writing *Pushing Up the Sky*, my motherhood memoir. The room where I wrote was unheated, and I wrapped the wool Pendleton blanket around me. I wrote the first draft to find the meaning. In the second, third, and fourth drafts, I put in everything I had left out. And then in the numerous drafts that followed, I took out everything that didn't fit, in order to make it sound like I just thought it up. These were long hours of writing, with my dog sleeping at my feet, a pot of pinto beans simmering on the back of the stove, and afternoon sun pouring through the window, with tiny dust particles floating in the sunlight. Early-morning rewriting and revising, while the cat walked on my keyboard. I wrote about the years when I had three kids, about my journey as their mother. The story of adopting my son from Korea and about my daughter being pushed from oldest to middle child when we brought a ten-year-old into our family and about my son growing up changed from cancer and a brain tumor—and how all of this taught me to let go of expectations and to forge a new identity.

In the indigo hours of early-morning writing, I always began with three pages of rough draft writing. But most of the time, I didn't save it. The process was the product—although Luke always said there is no product; it's all process.

Marie was no longer leading Bill's Friday morning writing class on a regular basis, but she dropped in sometimes. Another teacher stepped forward to lead the sessions. I continued on, along with Mary Lou, attending the classes that were filled with beginning and established writers, all in their seventies and eighties and a few over ninety. Everyone lovingly referred to me as the baby in the class.

Half of the writers had been longtime students of Bill's, and half of the class had never met Bill. They knew him only from our stories.

Each week we told stories about Bill. We brought him back, made him come alive for a few minutes on Friday mornings with our stories.

Frequently, a new writer joined our circle after hearing about us from one friend or another. For ten years after Bill's death, we gathered on Friday mornings, writing together and honoring Bill's legacy.

While I never developed personal friendships outside of class with many of these writers, I did form tight writer bonds with all of them. What I loved best was the opportunity to be within a large group of very old people, listening to them read their stories and gain a glimpse into their long lives.

Sometimes after class, I sat outside, in the same spot I had often sat with Bill. The sky was gray with clouds. It had rained the night before, and small stones lay beneath a half-inch of water in the gutter, near the bench we often sat on. The water and stones created ripples that reflected the sunlight like small mirrors.

I thought about all those times I had asked Bill, "What do I do with my book manuscript when the book is done?"

"You leave that part to me," he said. "First you've got to get it down on paper, and when you've got it finished, I'll see to it you find the right publisher."

I wasn't satisfied.

"But can't you just explain the book publishing process to me now?" I pressed.

I never did get an answer. From time to time, I'd ask again, and he always gave me a stare that said don't even think about it being published before you finish writing it.

23

MY YEARS AT THE SHELTER

Community work is a Native reciprocal value. In addition to my work as a writer, I needed to earn a stable income, and as often as possible, I made sure my employment was in line with my Native values. When I was offered a job at a youth crisis shelter group home and began working with runaway, homeless, at-risk, and foster youth in transition, I did not view this job offer as a coincidence. The child I had mothered for seven years had lived on the streets and in and out of multiple foster homes for this first ten years of her life. It was clear this was my path on my journey along the seven ways. I was invited to gain deeper compassion and understanding of what her life might have been like before she came into our family.

Although I didn't have any prior group home experience to my credit, I was the only one on the staff who was a mother, and I was the only one who was a member of a family of color. The kids who came into the shelter were Hispanic, white, Asian, mixed-race, and undocumented American Indian kids. A few of the kids were from upper- or middle-class homes, but most came from blue-collar families, and I was the only staff member with blue-collar lived experience. For the first time ever, it was my lack of privilege providing me with the necessary qualifications for the job.

My boss and the other staff members were in their late twenties and early thirties. Within my circle of elder woman friends, I was the youngest, and at the shelter I was the oldest.

Although my shift didn't begin until 8:00 a.m., I always arrived a bit early so that I had a few minutes to check in with the kids before they left for school. Opening the big white front door, the scent of coffee greeted me. There would be a plate of scrambled eggs or pancakes warming on the stove and a rush of teenagers stuffing books into backpacks. Girls with their faces pressed against the hallway full-length mirror checking details, making last-minute adjustments. When I first began working at the shelter, that's where I discovered my way in—getting to know the girls one on one, by doing what mothers say and do in the course of the getting-ready-for-school routine. Offering compliments, wishing them good luck on tests, helping the girls feel great about themselves as they began their day.

Usually, the boys slept longer and stumbled into the kitchen, leaving barely enough time to grab a pancake before they headed out the door to catch the bus. So, my opportunity to grab a quick chat with them needed to happen after school. Which is why I always stayed a few minutes longer after my shift ended in the afternoon.

The house, known as the "shelter," was located on a tree-lined street in a working-class neighborhood. It was impossible to drive by and guess this home was different than all of the other houses on the block, unless you watched the comings and goings, because it was a licensed residential group "home" to as many as eight kids between the ages of ten and seventeen on any given day. It was a long-established home, active in the community for over thirty-five years, and a trusted refuge and resource for youth and their families, with services available to the community twenty-four hours a day, 365 days a year. This meant an intake, meaning a new resident, might arrive in the middle of the night, so each morning brought a surprise to see who the newest resident might be.

There was a twenty-four-hour crisis hotline, and frequently, an intake began with a crisis call, though intakes could also stem from a drop-in visit from a youth, parent, or guardian and were also often precipitated by a phone call from Child Welfare Services or law enforcement. The phone rang constantly. An average stay at the shelter could last anywhere from three days to three months. Every word and deed was case noted and documented. At the beginning of our shift, we received changeover information so that we knew what had occurred all day and all night with the kids and within the house.

Consistency was key, with the staff working as a team, just like parents do in the best of families. It was a structured, family-like environment where the meals were home-cooked and everyone sat down together to eat. The kids did their own laundry, and schedules were posted. There was a daily house meeting; the kids had chores that rotated on a weekly basis. They could earn an allowance based on their behavior and level in the program. There was homework time in the afternoon, with a staff member available to offer help. After dinner a group activity took place, such as playing board games or watching a movie together.

Each day followed a planned routine because if you didn't keep the kids busy, they would keep you busy. It was the kind of family-like environment every child should be raised in, and it was a foreign world to the majority of the teens who were placed there for care.

My job was to serve as administrative assistant, to help with the volumes of office paperwork necessary for running a group home. Yet since I was working in an office that was situated just off the living room area, the boundaries between office paperwork and the kids became blurred. Although there were always two residential counselors slated to be on duty on each shift, there were days when one had to drive a child to a doctor or dentist appointment and the other had called in sick and I was needed to assist with the children.

What I knew then about parenting was gleaned from raising three kids. I'm also an instinctive mother, with lots of hard-won experience. But I didn't know everything I needed to know, and the weekly staff training sessions were a favorite part of my week. The new language communication skills I was acquiring brought me to a deeper, better level of communication with the kids in the shelter and within my own family.

I looked forward to getting up in the morning and going to work. My office life at the shelter, with the constant noise and interruptions, was delightful. It reminded me of home. The pattern with the clatter of kids nearby was exactly like my work as a writer while also being a mother when my three children were growing up.

I worked on reports and filed paperwork, all the while keeping a keen eye and ear tuned so I could catch any mischief or heartrending moments when a child needed extra attention.

Each day, instead of taking my ten-minute break and lunch hour alone, I chose to spend my time with the kids. When you work in a residential home youth crisis shelter, there are always at least one or two kids in the house at any time of the day needing a snack or needing someone to listen.

Because life goes on, even when you live at a shelter, there are intimate moments etched in my heart forever. The high school boy I grew fond of, ironing his shirt, getting ready to go to his senior prom, poking his head into my office door, beaming, showing me his new jacket. The snatches of conversation between us on an important day in his life, like mother and son, only we were not.

The sixteen-year-old American Indian girl I had grown fond of, discovering that she loves to write, has a talent for it, her writing short stories and poems and asking me to read them.

There was the teen girl I'd formed a bond with who had grown up in one of the toughest of tough situations, with gang activity, a mean girl, a hard girl, and she let her guard down around the house, showing her soft spots, losing her edge, turning into a darn good cook and becoming a caring, generous person on her good days.

The one thing you can always count on in a shelter is change. Beginnings and endings, someone arriving and someone leaving. Staff did their best to make sure there was closure when it was time for a child to leave. If they knew ahead of time, a special dinner would be prepared. There is never an easy way to say goodbye to the kids you treasure, which is why I felt sad each time a difficult kid left and everyone in the house was glad to see them go.

After a thorny child departed, the other kids had a wonderful way of banding together—dropping their defenses and coming together as one cohesive group, and for a day or two, life at the shelter would be easy and smooth. Then another child would arrive or leave, and the cycle turned again.

Although I imagined working at the shelter until I was a very old woman, one day it was my turn to leave. The economy had changed, funding was tight, and in a budget meeting, a decision was made to eliminate my position.

On my last day I found a cake awaiting me, baked in my honor. A few of the kids and all of my coworkers presented me with home-made cards; each one carried a paragraph or two of sincere words recounting warm and funny memories. This was something the shelter was famous for: the personal touch of always assembling their own homemade thank-you, birthday, and goodbye cards.

At the end of my shift, before I walked out the door, I sat on the floor for a few minutes with a couple of the kids I had close relation-ship with. We sat cross-legged in a circle, and we said our goodbyes.

Tears streamed down the face of the toughest–of–tough situations girl, the former hard girl who had begun to let her guard down. Then she said: "Each one of us will leave here eventually—we're all just passing through. At first I thought I'd hate it here, and I still want to leave, but instead, I've decided to make the most of my time here."

Perhaps it is wishful thinking, but I believe I saw a glimmer of hope in her eyes, and her sense of what is possible had been expanded. She had been able to let herself cry, instead of hiding her pain behind sharp words, and that was a good enough start for me.

Before I left, I spent a few minutes wishing the kids good luck on homework assignments they had completed and helping them feel great about themselves as they began their night.

Although I didn't want to leave, most of all I am thankful for the opportunity I was given. And every night since, I've been thanking my lucky stars and am filled with deep gratitude for the years I spent at the shelter.

24

THE WINTER IT CAME BACK

After my job at the youth crisis shelter ended, I took the summer off to be with the kids and to finish writing my memoir. The book was done, Vanessa and Jay were back in school, and I planned to do freelance writing for a while before searching for another job.

In November, two weeks before Jay's fifteenth birthday, I realized something was wrong, very wrong. I followed Jay into the bathroom and watched him open the medicine cabinet and reach for the bottle of Advil.

"Do you have a headache again?" I asked.

He shrugged his shoulders, then hiccupped hard and ducked his head in the toilet and threw up. He wretched until his stomach heaved in frantic dry spasms. Tears welled in Jay's eyes. For the past two days he had been having headaches off and on. I sank into the deep, silent panic that made me calm. I knew the brain tumor was back.

Our primary care physician called in an authorization for an MRI. Jay hid the fear he felt behind a mask of quiet strength.

Each day, as often as I could, I kept my eyes on Jay. I memorized his every move. I watched him talk on the phone with friends, snuck side-glances while he did his homework and as he sprinted out the door to go to school. In the middle of the night, I poked my head into his room, and I could hear him hiccupping, steady, quiet hiccups that didn't interrupt his sleep.

That week Jay was elected student of the month, and he got a lead part in the school play. I tried to continue on as usual, until the MRI confirmed my worst fear—the tumor was back, an anaplastic ependymoma, and this time its fingers spread into the brainstem.

We had to decide on a plan of treatment. We contacted the surgeon who had performed Jay's first brain tumor surgery. Surgery was scheduled.

Luck held—most of the tumor was successfully resected. In less than a week, Jay was out of the hospital, recovering well. But what to do about the remaining brain tumor slivers that were inoperable? He had *already* received his lifetime dose of whole-brain radiation, and the chemotherapy drugs he used with the first diagnosis offered little hope of curing a recurrent tumor. There was a small chance that stereotactic radio surgery might be of some help in stalling the tumor's growth. We set up a consultation and began the treatment plan.

On Christmas Eva a large box filled with one thousand paper cranes arrived in the mail. Good luck cranes. A friend of Jay's had made a plea to all of her friends and posted a notice on an origami website, asking them to fold paper cranes for Jay. She enclosed the original envelopes the paper cranes had arrived in. The postmarks were from all over the United States, along with paper cranes from Denmark, Holland, Korea, and Germany.

The paper birds arrived folded flat, pre-strung, and ready to hang. We had golden cranes, cranes on fancy green paper with pink parasols on it, cranes made in brilliant blues, yellow, and orange. A few of the cranes were folded with cherry blossom paper, and some were bright-green neon cranes. Some were folded from newsprint, and others were glow-in-the-dark cranes. Twenty cranes were made from paper with tiny Korean flags. Crimson, purple, and magenta, a rainbow of paper cranes.

As we unfolded each tiny wing and strung the paper cranes from a skinny oak branch, we could feel a thousand good wishes encircle Jay. Each paper crane was a loving tribute. We could feel the power, precision, and devotion in the folding, the unfolding, of each wing, a prayer. We could also feel the link reaching back to Sadako Sasaki, the now-famous little girl who developed acute leukemia ten years after being exposed to radiation during the atomic bombing of Hiroshima. Inspired by the Japanese story that anyone who makes one thousand origami cranes will see their wish come true. Sadako spent her last days folding paper cranes on her hospital bed in the hope she would recover.

As we strung the cranes, I thought about the jingle dress story. The story is that the dress was first seen in a dream. A medicine man's granddaughter grew sick, and as he slept, his spirit guides came to him and told him to make a Jingle dress for her. They said if she danced in it, the dress would heal her. The jingle dress was made, and the tribe came together to watch her dance. At first she was too sick to dance on her own, and so her tribe carried her, but after a little time, she was able to dance on her own.

I encouraged Jay and Vanessa to continue on with their ordinary routines, to live as normally as possible. Someone from the PTA at Jay's school called and wanted me to contribute a dessert for a bake sale. I didn't tell her Jay had a brain tumor; instead, I agreed to bake cookies.

Usually, Jay rose to our household dessert challenges. He enjoyed cooking and baking. He got out the baking sheets, the eggs, and measured out the flour, and then he ran out of energy and directed my efforts to produce his perfected chocolate chip cookie recipe. I placed three cookies in each plastic bag, tied them with purple ribbons, and delivered them to the bake sale.

I felt like I was on some kind of an emotional layaway plan: experience life now and feel it later.

Most of the time I forced myself to stay in the moment and didn't allow myself the luxury of worrying about the future. A future without Jay in it was impossible to imagine.

I watched Jay thumb through the newspaper.

"So why do you suppose when a person dies from cancer, they say he lost the battle?" Jay questioned. His face was pinched with confusion. "Don't worry, Mom, I know dying is not about losing." And with the zeal of a kid determined to restore order to the universe, he announced, "Heaven is filled with winners."

Having a positive attitude was important to Jay. Although he had very low energy, he attended school for half-days because he loved school. He helped his friends understand that it's important not to think of cancer in terms of winning or losing. For Jay cancer was a journey he must make, and he intended to live as well as possible and to be kind. He taught me that a cancer journey is also about loving more than you ever thought possible.

Somehow that winter Vanessa managed to take driver's education and got her driver's license. I attempted to win her confidence by allowing her to drive me to the grocery store. Her capable hands gripped the steering wheel. I pressed myself into the passenger seat and clutched the armrest, my shoulders riding up.

"You aren't very relaxed," she observed. When the errand was completed and she pulled our car into the driveway, I was thankful, and my mind burst into quiet relief.

Feathers from a crow were scattered on the front lawn. Recently, a friend told me he needed more crow feathers to finish making new powwow dance regalia. I went into the house to call him, then came back out and sat down on the front porch steps. The sun glowed gold and then deep red. I watched the sky for a long time. The air smelled of woodsmoke. Each breath I took smelled rich like the ground after a rainstorm. I watched the bats come out; they dipped and dived through the now dusky sky. It was quiet except for the crickets.

Three months later, in February, Jay continued to feel reasonably well. He held life in his two hands and was squeezing out its sweetest juices. On good days he made himself a cup of cocoa, poured cold cereal into a bowl, and sat at the white tile breakfast bar, eating and reading. The best days were when he didn't vomit. I kept the garbage disposal side of the sink empty, just in case. Brain tumors aren't like the flu. There wasn't any nausea, no warning, just a sudden wave.

Even when he did throw up, he possessed complete goodwill and wholehearted forgiveness. He cleaned himself up, and a few minutes later he would go back to his meal.

He didn't complain about having a brain tumor; he moved forward with his life. As ill as he was, he gave the impression he'd outlive all of us. But suddenly, in March, his voice grew raspy.

"It's really weird," Jay said. "I just completely run out of breath." The next day Jay had difficulty swallowing, and it was beginning to be hard for him to talk. His chest rattled when he breathed.

Jay was admitted to the hospital. The doctor came to talk with us. In a semiprivate hospital room, we conversed in low private whispers, while Jay's roommate, a sixteen-year-old boy who was an appendectomy patient, thumbed through pages of a sports magazine, pretending disinterest, giving us the illusion of privacy.

The news wasn't good. An MRI showed that the tumor was three times as big, and Jay's body was beginning to shut down. I blinked in surprise. Jay knit his brow as he let the news sink in. Gary and I sat feeling helpless while he was placed on oxygen and a feeding tube was inserted.

"I'm not afraid to die," Jay said. "I just don't want to do it. But if it turns out that I have to, then I want to die at home."

I made a quick phone call to hospice and left a message for someone to call me back. Someone from hospice came to talk with us, and then for SIX HOURS we waited for the hospital paperwork to be competed, allowing Jay to leave. By now he could barely speak, his words were slurred, yet he was completely alert and fully coherent. He wrote notes when he wanted to tell us something.

I watched Jay's face, studied the tiny dark mole on the top of his right ear, and memorized the way his black hair shined red in sunlight from the window. It was the only thing I knew to do. It was not hard to talk to Jay about cancer. But I wondered how long it would be before he couldn't hear me anymore. I thought about the day when his body began to wear out, about the day when he stopped living.

Before Jay was released from the hospital, a nurse came to remove his feeding tube. Jay frowned, and he wrote me a note that said, "After they take it out, how am I going to eat?" Gary blinked back tears. My mouth remained open as I searched for a reply. I took a deep breath of hospital air that smelled of old wax and disinfectant.

"As your body begins to slow down, you probably won't be feeling hungry," I offered. We faced each other, not two feet apart yet in different universes. Jay stiffened, drew back from me, then he punched me in the arm, hard.

A second later he pulled me close to him and gave me a light kiss on the cheek.

"We can ask them to leave the tube in," I suggested, "just in case you get hungry."

Twelve hours later, Jay was settled in at home. The dog gave him a welcome home lick. A hospice nurse arrived and taught me how to care for Jay. I learned to operate the oxygen tanks. There were so many dials and valves and coils and hoses that at first it seemed too complicated. Frosty air escaped the overflow valve. Although I corrected the problem almost immediately, Jay's dark intelligent eyes regarded me with raw suspicion.

Usually, it was Jay who taught *me* how to make things work. He programmed the VCR, he installed computer programs, and on driving trips he read the map and gave *me* directions. He was patient; he always took his time making sure things were exactly right. Suddenly, time had been transformed from a resource into an unseen opponent.

We used the swabs hospice provided with cool water and a bit of mint so Jay's mouth would feel fresh and clean. He relaxed when he realized the hospice nurse wouldn't be poking him with needles as so many others had already done in the hospital. Jay had grown to hate the hospital; he was able to live so much more at home. At home everything was peaceful and familiar. We placed a hospital bed in the living room, and the cord on his oxygen was long enough so that he could move about and relax on the couch, allowing him to hear everything going on in the kitchen. Through the wall of windows stretching across the living room, we watched the sky fall dark and fill with stars.

Gary, Vanessa, and I curled up with Jay on the couch; all of us cuddled together in that tight space. I watched Jay's face, and through the window I watched for shooting stars.

"Do you want me to sleep out here with you tonight?" I asked, thinking that amid all the oxygen tubes, the strange surrounding of the hospital bed in our living room, Jay would feel lonely and scared. His eyes lit up, and he squeezed my hand. Dressed in sweats, I settled myself at his side.

In the morning he felt well enough to be concerned about an online order he'd placed, and he wanted me to check to see if it had shipped.

Although he had very low energy and napped off and on all day, when he was awake, he was fully alert. He could no longer talk at all and communicated by writing notes to us, yet his jet-black eyes spoke volumes.

At four o'clock Vanessa came home from school. Then a friend dropped by. They played a game of checkers, and Jay won the game. They watched television for a while, and then Jay said he had a headache. Morphine needed to be administered every six to eight hours for pain, yet all day Jay had remained pain free, so I hadn't given him any.

I put on my glasses and carefully measured out one tiny drop. I practiced twice, to make sure I had the right amount, and each time I let the liquid drip back into the bottle from the eyedropper. I gave Jay the tiny drop of morphine and helped him into bed, and he fell asleep with the dog curled near the foot of the bed.

Vanessa left to go to a school choir rehearsal, and Gary and I sat near Jay's bed talking softly. A few minutes later I leaned over to check on Jay. I put my hand on his arm, and my stomach froze tight; I could feel him slipping away.

"Squeeze my finger if you can hear me," I pleaded. Jay gave my finger a light squeeze, so weightless I could barely feel it. He slept in a classic fetal position, knees beneath his chest, occupying as small a space as possible. A few minutes later I spoke to Jay again, and this time no response. Fear unraveled inside me. Gently, I grabbed his wrist with my thumb and forefinger and counted a pulse.

At first I thought I must have given Jay too much morphine. Gary called hospice, and the nurse insisted that I hadn't. It was an irrational feeling of me thinking of things I could have done differently that might have resulted in Jay being fully alert again.

Hospice offered to send someone over, but we preferred support by telephone.

Gary tried to telephone Vanessa to tell her to come home right away, but he was unable to reach her.

All evening we sat at Jay's bedside. Then his breathing stopped, and at that moment Vanessa walked in the door.

"I had a feeling that I needed to come home," she said, "so I left right in the middle of choir rehearsal." Vanessa dropped her coat in the hall; she put her hand on Jay's chest and spoke to her brother. His eyebrows arched, but he didn't respond in any other way, yet we felt positive he could hear her. She folded herself onto the bed with him.

A few minutes later Gary and I climbed onto the bed too. Jay lay in the center among the three of us, small, quiet, immobile, with his dog at his side. Soon after, he fell into a coma, yet we felt positive he could still hear us.

All night Jay's breathing stopped and then started again.

"Maybe we need to tell him that's it's okay to die," Vanessa offered.

"Jay, I love you," she said. "Don't worry, I'll do your chores and help Mom. Time is different in heaven; we'll be there with you before you know it," she cooed.

Gary and I sat with our arms around each other and tears pouring down our cheeks.

I kissed Jay on his forehead. "It's okay," I whispered. "Don't wait for anything—it's time for you to go."

We huddled around Jay and wished him a good journey as he crossed over to the other side. At that moment he smiled the sweetest smile, and a peaceful feeling as wide as the sky settled over us. Something warm and cozy fell across my heart. And then he was gone.

Rain began to fall, pounding the roof. As quick as it had arrived, the warm, cozy feeling left. Gary, Vanessa, and I agreed, it was as though a million years had passed. As if we had traveled with Jay beyond this life. We didn't wonder; we knew we had gone all the way to the point of entry with him. We didn't see the light; we felt it surround us. It pulled us, drew us in. For the briefest moment I wanted Jay to go. It felt right, like the most natural thing in the world. In that moment I was certain he was headed home.

Jay had only been gone for a few minutes, and we were plunged back to earth into a stark awareness that no longer held a living, breathing Jay Trevor. Jay's body lay still and small, and we sat with his body in the hush just before dawn, when darkness gives way to light. The peaceful smile on his face was preserved like a monument. I sat stroking his hands, tracing the creases in his palm.

As I held his hand, I thought about my great-great-grandma. My dad had grown up with her, and through the stories she told, it was as if I'd known her too. She had given birth to eleven babies. The first died at four months, the second at age eight. It went on like that for years, Grandma giving birth and Grandpa making baby boards, digging holes, and lowering those dead babies into the ground. It was a time of measles and small pox epidemic for American Indian people.

My mind glimpsed my great-great-grandma, and I felt a distant memory pulling me back. I could hear her wailing like wind coming up, crying, swaying. I thought about how her cries probably drifted into the cabins of nearby white settlers, and I wondered if they knew the high, shrill sounds pressing against the night were from an Indian mother mourning her dead child.

Decisions about the removal of Jay's body had to be made. Although I knew I had to, I couldn't bear to call the funeral home and have them come take him away.

Gary made the phone call, and another miracle surfaced: the funeral director, though we did not know him personally, said that his church prayer line had been praying for Jay all night. He agreed to let us bring Jay's body to the mortuary ourselves. We wrapped him in the blue flannel sheets from his bed patterned with tiny snowmen. Vanessa drove because she wanted to drive. Gary was in no shape, and I couldn't do it. I sat in the passenger seat, and Gary sat in the back with Jay's body wrapped in a bundle on his lap. We were lucky to be granted that one small grace, to take Jay's body to the funeral home ourselves.

I felt the boundary of time collapse around me again, like it did when Luke died. As if it had been one very long day since greeting one-year-old baby Jay at the airport when he arrived from Korea. In the blink of an eye, fourteen years had passed, allowing me the privilege of being his mother, and now night was setting in, closing Jay's life in a full circle.

All that day a long, steady stream of people came to our house. I had wanted to be still and quiet, to keep that peaceful feeling we all felt as Jay was walking on inside me for as long as possible. But I couldn't because friends and family came to comfort us. I have no idea who was here; I wish I could remember who came.

In the days after Jay died, I didn't want to have to behave in a normal manner and make attempts at conversation. I wanted to wail, to rock back and forth, moaning and sobbing.

There is a Paiute mourning ritual known as the Cry Dance, wherein the dancers and singers, clutching strips of clothing that belonged to the person who has died, support the bereft as she fills the silence for a few minutes with her "cry"—the sound of human grief. I wished that a Cry Dance could be held for me because acting as if I had the ability to hold it all together was more than I could bear.

I wished to find someone with knowledge of Cherokee or Lenape or Seneca death rituals and traditions. It would have helped to carry me, but I didn't have the strength to go searching. The only tradition I knew about was the cutting of hair, and I cut off my long hair.

I was taught that our hair is a physical manifestation of our spirit. Many tribes respect the tradition of cutting off your hair when someone close to you dies. It's an outward symbol of the deep sadness we feel and a physical reminder of the loss. The cut hair represents the time with their loved one, which is now over, and the new growth is the life after.

I got through those first days minutes at a time. My chest ached so much, there were moments when I thought I might die from heartbreak. We were all doing the best we could. The world had been knocked out from under us, and we were free-falling.

The rain continued all week, and the roof began to leak in multiple places. The largest drip fell exactly above where Jay's hospital bed had sat in the living room. If he were still in that bed, the rain would have dripped on his pillow.

One evening, a few days later, we sat in the living room watching television, and I felt a tap on the top of my head. I turned around to look, and there wasn't anyone behind me. I wasn't in the mood to be teased and had a feeling of someone sneaking up on me. I kept whipping my head around to catch Gary or Vanessa in the act, yet they were both engrossed in the show and hadn't moved off the couch. I had the oddest feeling of someone else being in the room with us.

"What's the matter?" Gary asked.

"Someone just tapped me on the head," I admitted.

"We're watching Jay's favorite show," Vanessa announced. "It must have been him." She was joking, of course. But we also believed it was Jay.

A few minutes later I felt another tap on my head.

"Hey," I said. "It happened again."

When we left the house to go somewhere, after we got back home, we felt an odd sensation, as if Jay had gone with us. But obviously, he hadn't.

Condolence cards fanned out on the table. On the bookshelf there was a photograph of me, taken by Jay, in which I'm standing in the ocean. When I looked at this picture, I remembered the grin on Jay's face, the mischievous look in his eye, and the wave that washed over me seconds after the snapshot was taken. I remember Jay laughing hard, and his laughter made me laugh. It reminded me of the time when I borrowed Jay's knee-high rubber boots.

I was padding my way through ankle-deep water, crossing the creek.

"Be careful, Mom," Jay shouted from the other bank. His voice was low, and I could tell he was trying hard not to laugh. At once I felt the gush of icy water melt into my sock.

A palpable energy hovered in Jay's voice. "I forgot to tell you—there is a hole in the left boot," he said.

Memorial service planning began. The pastor of our Korean church had retired, and it had been a while since I last spoke with him. We picked up right where we left off, as if no amount of time had passed. His white hair shone in the morning sun, and wildflowers bloomed in the field behind us as we made our plans.

Vanessa and Reverend Lee gave a eulogy at Jay's memorial service, and everyone we had ever known, from every aspect of our lives, was present. Jay's friends, their parents, his teachers. Vanessa's friends and their parents. Our friends, our neighbors. All of our family members.

A friend sang "Amazing Grace" in Korean, and Korean elders said prayers in the Korean language. If ceremonies are the heart of a culture, then language is the lifeblood. A calm washed over me I hadn't felt in days.

So many people came to pay their respects, everyone couldn't fit inside the chapel, so the guests spilled outside into the courtyard and out on the grass. Scanning the crowd, I saw the faces of everybody I knew, even those who had to drive for miles. We laughed and cried together, and one by one, we hugged each of them. Another friend captured all those hugs and tears on video.

After the memorial service a large group of family and friends came to our home, where more friends were already gathered preparing food. Marie brought out her homemade salsa and frybread. Mary Lou's famous deviled eggs were on the table, and she was cutting up apples for a fruit salad.

The sun came out, and we filled the yard with people laughing and weeping. A basketball game was in process, and someone pulled out the checkerboard. It was the kind of gathering Jay liked best; he would have enjoyed the day, and who knows, maybe he did.

A few days later we went out on the *Star Dust*, the boat Jay always fished from, and we scattered his ashes in the ocean, in the spot where he once caught a thirty-eight-pound halibut.

25

WITH NOTHING AHEAD
BUT SKY

I awoke at 3:00 a.m. The night air was thick with skunk, clear and cool. I got out of bed and sat before the window looking out into the dark shapes of trees. The moon, in a corner of the sky, was full and wide and my thoughts heavy saddlebags. I pulled a coat over my nightgown and walked out into the damp air and squeezed out the tears. A spiderweb stretched across the path. I paused sleepily, listening to the thin riffs of crickets.

All of a sudden it occurred to me that Jay's birth family had no way of knowing he was dead. What if they should decide to come forward and try to locate him?

In the morning I contacted a friend in Korea and faxed her a copy of the eulogy Reverend Lee had given at Jay's memorial service, written in Hangul. Then I gave her the address and asked her to write a letter and send it to Sun Rak Won, the orphanage where Jay had lived for the first year of his life. The eulogy Reverend Lee wrote, saying he thought of Jay as his own grandchild, gave a personal glimpse into our lives.

In less than a week, I received an email response from the orphanage letting me know my correspondence had been placed in Jay's file.

I had done all that I could for Jay. I felt a lump in my throat knowing one day his birthmother might learn of his death, and then, at that moment, her grieving for him would begin with piercing raw aching, the kind of pain and sorrow that now surrounded me. Then the gap opened for me, and I saw fully and felt the grief journey that began for her the moment Jay was born. He was born in a small rural farming village in South Korea, and he was born with his fingers, on both hands, tightly fused together. Soon after we adopted him, he endured multiple skin graphs and surgeries to separate his fingers.

By the time he was four years old, he had ten perfect fingers. His hands and fingers were greatly scarred, but his fingers functioned perfectly, and he had excellent dexterity.

I imagined how his Korean mother must have prayed for a miracle when he was born. Of the despair holding her hostage the morning she left him at the orphanage and the searing pain she must have felt each day waking up in the morning without him.

The days after Jay's death rolled by faster than I wanted them to, taking me farther away from my son. My heart folded over each time new acquaintances asked me the question, "How many children do you have?"

What felt most isolating, Gary, Vanessa, and I agreed, was that without Jay in our family circle, we didn't have anything or anyone to identify us as Asian. New people in our lives would never guess that in the center of our hearts we were connected to Korean ethnicity.

In the summer, before Jay got sick, I had received a phone call from Robert Bensen, telling me he was editing an anthology, a collection of Native American voices on child custody and education, and he invited me to contribute a chapter to the book. I sent in my submission, and it was accepted.

The book Bob was editing was *Children of the Dragonfly: Native American Voices on Child Custody and Education.* Native American children had a long history of being removed from their homes for placement in residential schools and placed for adoption with white families, and this was the first anthology to document this struggle for cultural survival on both sides of the U.S. and Canadian border. The anthology included the works of contemporary Native authors Joy Harjo, Luci Tapahonso, Eric Gansworth, and Sherman Alexie, along with classic

Native writers Zitkala-Sa and E. Pauline Johnson, with contributions from twenty important new writers as well, including me. Our essays took readers from the boarding school movement of the 1870s to the Sixties Scoop in Canada and the Indian Child Welfare Act of 1978 in the United States. The stories also shined a spotlight on the tragic consequences of racist practices, suppression of Indian identity in government schools, and the campaign against Indian childbearing through involuntary sterilization.

As a writer, it was a great milestone to have my work included, and the great joy I felt being a contributor carried me through the difficult months while my son was struggling to live with a brain tumor, and it carried me through his death.

However, two weeks after Jay died, I receive a phone call from Bob saying the publisher had cut my piece, and they wanted me to write a different piece based on one single sentence within my essay. The new story they wanted me to write was an account of adopting a Korean child, about the struggles of his adoption packed into the spaces between *Korean* and *Native American* and *American*.

I told Bob my son had died two weeks ago and that I was wading through deep grief and sorrow and didn't think I could write anything. Within our conversation, somehow, I found strength when Bob promised to guide me through the writing. In the process of discussing the topic I would write on, I told him much of what he wanted me to contribute could be pulled from a book manuscript, a memoir sitting in my desk drawer. Bob held my hand while I waded deeper into emotionally charged territory, and we developed a close friendship while I revised a chapter from *Pushing Up the Sky*, and it was included in *Children of the Dragonfly*, published in 2021.

I will always be thankful I was able to pull myself up to write the chapter for *Dragonfly*. My story in the book about my connection with the Korean community and how Korean ethnicity was braided into my life gave back to me a portion of my lost heart. The publication of the book also opened many doors for me, and the book is now in its second edition and has been adopted for classroom use at a number of universities.

After completing the chapter for Dragonfly, I didn't write anything for months. After Jay died, things just kept growing more difficult. Next, our dog, Sadie, the rock of our family, our cherished Newfoundland now grown old, began having difficulty breathing. Her chest rattled, and she gasped for air. We took her to the vet, he checked her over, and then he told us what we already knew. Instead, we went home to think it over.

Vanessa gave Sadie a spoonful of vanilla ice cream. Sadie slurped at it with puppylike zest. We petted and cuddled her. My memory recalls Jay being with us that day, only he couldn't have been.

Later in the afternoon, when Sadie was getting worse, we knew it was time to let her go. The vet arranged for us to have a room to ourselves for as long as we needed. I knelt down by Sadie and gently stroked her. We petted her as the overdose of anesthesia made its swift deadly way. Outside the vet's office we stood weeping.

This time grief and sorrow lodged in Vanessa's jaw. The dentist had her wear a mouth splint day and night. For weeks she lived on blender drinks and smoothies. She was irritable and hair-triggered. The sound of her unhappiness ranged from yelling to extended crying. Sunlight glittered in from the window. I watched her greet the morning by making noise, banging the blender on the counter as she prepared her breakfast.

"Hey," I said, using my most soothing tone of voice.

"I've lost so much weight," she snapped. "None of my jeans fit me."

I put my hand on the small of her back; she was thin as an arrow; her hip bones looked sharp enough to push through the soft folds of her jeans. That's when I wanted to burst into tears because I knew I couldn't buy her a smaller size pair, not this month anyway.

The stream of sun from the window grew diffuse, and the early-morning warmth was gone. The room felt cold. I made myself a cup of coffee and began my day. I confronted the refrigerator. We were low on milk, but there were plenty of eggs. I thought about frying up a couple and then changed my mind; better save the eggs to make an omelet for dinner.

Usually, Vanessa bought many of her own clothes from money she earned babysitting. But recently, I'd insisted she cut back on her work hours. The flu hit her hard twice since Jay died, and she needed extra rest. Still, lack of money seemed a silly reason not to buy her a new pair of jeans. When Jay was terminally ill from cancer, I bought him a new pair of sweatpants, knowing he'd only need them for a short time.

I was tired of thinking about money, but my stomach clenched around the words anyway. At least I was working again, yet business was slow for Gary now, and we were back to making ends meet. Living on a tight budget didn't usually bother me, though there had been more expenses than usual lately, a new roof on the house and car repair expenses. I didn't care about luxury, just as long as I could pay the utility bills, buy groceries, and still have enough money left over to buy new pants for my kids when they shrank to a smaller size.

I finished my coffee and blinked back tears. Poor Vanessa not only lost her brother to death; she also lost her parents to grief. Though I wished I had the power to uplift Vanessa, I didn't. I was barely coping. Gary couldn't do it either; he clung with all his might to hang on to his own sanity. We tried, but we didn't have much within us to help each other. I imagined us each in a tiny rowboat, drifting alone, in a stormy sea.

Now I am able to see that in our first year of bereavement, we were right where we were supposed to be, but I didn't know it at the time. Luckily, I never felt like denying myself pleasure, not even in the first few weeks or months. I still tried to watch movies and read books and walk on the beach. In a grief support group, I met a mother who said she didn't want to laugh or eat delicious food or go anywhere out of respect for her dead child. That mother also said her anger was so raging, she couldn't even stand to see the flowers blooming in her yard. She said, "How dare those flowers blare open to face the sun." She wanted to put weed killer on them so they would look as bad as she was feeling. I'd discovered that type of reaction was fairly common, and I was grateful my grief didn't lead me down that path.

Fortunately, we had a wide network of family and friends to keep us shored up. We managed as well as it is possible to manage so soon after the death of a son and brother. Gary and I went to work; we remembered to pay the utility bills and checked the oil level in the car. Vanessa kept her grades up, and I helped her fill out college applications. She had planned to go away to school, yet after Jay died, she wanted to give the idea up and attend a college close to home. Even though I would have liked to keep Vanessa near me, in my heart I knew it was best to help her stick with her original plan and to follow her dreams.

My plans for parenthood sat like scenery on an empty stage. I wasn't ready to have an empty nest, yet I didn't want Vanessa to feel she had to stay home because of me. She needed the experience of living on a college campus full-time, and I needed to come up with a new life for myself. But how could I choose my destiny when I couldn't even buy a new sweater without exchanging it twice before deciding on a color and the right fit? I was starting my life over from scratch, and I was terrified of making decisions, even little ones.

I didn't think I would ever care about anything ever again. My mind felt glued shut, and my heart was beginning to feel like it was laminated, sealed in plastic to keep out further pain. Then I had a soul-bleaching moment when I understood that I didn't want to stay closed up and hollow feeling forever. There had to be a way to allow myself the space and time to grieve deep and fully, to feel every ounce of the pain, and yet continue to walk forward. Jay, a pole star in my life, had passed. I would never get over it. Nor would I ever be the same. I would not give up or give in to society's mistaken notion of getting over grief fast in order to get on with my life. I would find a way to learn to live with grief and not allow it to hold me back.

The answer came when I remembered a family vacation to the state of Washington. We went to Mount St. Helens, and Jay and I stared at the way she looked years after her summit was removed by a volcanic eruption.

That day I stood watching the slate-blue dusk blend into ragged peaks and lava domes. A friend once had a cabin perched on a bluff overlooking the lake, surrounded by gigantic pines. I pulled up the hood of my sweatshirt, my face strained into the wind. Fireweed and purple-red flowers dotted the level earthen floor in a place where a forest and the cabin once stood. We walked, circling the crater, and I saw wild violets blooming.

The mountain had been scattered and sundered into bits, and she survived. I swallowed a clotty grief deep inside my throat. A grief so wide it gave me laryngitis. Bold and enthusiastic thoughts of Jay filled me. I was breathing proof he was once more than a photograph.

I shuffled out into the empty field of my mind to find enough words to make it through another winter of writing. Nothing quits. My life had changed into something I didn't want, and I began gathering the pieces that were left of me and coaxing them into growth. I was starting out again, but like the mountain, I'd lost all of my big trees.

The horizon was still mine. I felt myself part of the mountain, with hills catching the sunset through a furious wind, dust devils kicking up dirt. All my senses became alive, out on the edge. I imagined fireweed blooming on the burned-over land in my heart, beginning purple petals.

We had completed a long year of firsts: my first Mother's Day without Jay and Gary's first Father's Day. We moved through Jay's sixteenth birthday without him.

Even though rituals were important to me, we had no idea how to observe the first anniversary of Jay's death—the day his soul returned from where it came. We spent every day remembering Jay, so I didn't see how it made sense to designate the actual date of his death for this purpose. Wasn't it better to celebrate his fifteen years on earth every day of our lives?

My mind was centering on these thoughts the afternoon Vanessa began begging me to buy her a pair of red satin pants. Gary was with us, and we were at a bargain outlet mall.

"But these pants are marked way down," Vanessa pleaded.

"Where on earth would you wear them?" I queried. "It would make sense if you wanted to get them for a special occasion, but where would you go in them?"

"I'm alive, Mom," Vanessa said. "I could wear them whenever I was in the mood to wear them. If I woke up and felt like putting on these wonderful red pants and wearing them to school, then I could do it because I'm alive!"

Gary and I looked at each other. We both had tears in our eyes. We looked at Vanessa. She had tears in her eyes too. Gary then tossed the red pants into our shopping cart, and we three stood in the middle of the store crying until we started laughing.

Thus, a tradition began. In our family the day Jay died has become the day each year when we renew our vows to be kind and gentle with ourselves, to treat ourselves and each other well, to honor each other because we are still alive. We're still here, living and loving, and that's what life is all about.

26

SOMEWHERE SOUTHWEST
OF THE MIDDLE

Two weeks before leaving for college, Vanessa brought home a puppy. She was working as a camp counselor at Camp Ronald McDonald, where eleven puppies were born during the summer. The puppies were eight weeks old, and the camp staff knew they had to find homes for them.

"I'm not sure I'm ready for another dog." I groaned.

"You'll be lonely without me," Vanessa cooed.

I followed her outside with the pup. The day was bright and sunny, with the faint colors of autumn emerging in the scrub oak. I looked at my daughter and saw the totality of her—the first time I saw her face in the hospital delivery room, the first time I held her in my arms, her first sentence. I remembered her at age four, walking into her bedroom at the first light of dawn and finding her wearing only a black velvet beret and nylon fairy wings with loose elastic straps looped over her shoulders.

"I'm going to a party," she whispered. "Would you like to come?" Her barely slept-in pajamas would be discovered later, when I searched the narrow space between the bed and the wall.

She was about to leave home and move onto a college campus hundreds of miles away. While I was happy for her and had greatly encouraged her to go away to college, instead of attending our local university, the usually tiny cyst on my ankle had begun swelling to peach size, just like it had when we found out that Jay had the second brain tumor, when the cancer turned terminal, four months before he died.

In a wholly new way, I was thrilled to see my daughter, for the first time in months since her brother departed this world, take charge of what she wanted. Which at the moment meant she wanted me to have this dog. I watched her, tanned skin, rolling her too-serious eyes, car keys in her hand. I could not gather back one moment of her childhood, only marvel at what would come next.

I felt my old self crawl out from under an imagined rock. It began to dawn on me that I was delighted. She was the perfect dog, mountain born, mixed breed, calm, and going to be big.

"I'm going to call her Jenny," I announced. I cradled the puppy and nuzzled her soft neck. I felt her heart thumping, her breath quick and marvelous.

27

COMING BACK TO
THE WORLD

Vanessa was off at college, and in the second year after Jay's death, some of our friends hinted that it had been long enough and that we should be getting on with our lives. It had become painfully clear that "getting on with our lives" to some people meant avoiding Jay's name in conversations. This irked me. A person can sell their medical practice and retire, and forever after, they will be referred to as "Doctor." Yet there were those who viewed motherhood spent on a child who had died as an era that should no longer be acknowledged.

We were getting on with our lives. We had the new dog. Gary and I had established a pattern of watching the sun set together each evening. On weekends he still fished, and he'd begun to make a wider circle of fishing friends in the Japanese community. I was still writing. Vanessa was off at college. Each of us, in our own way, was establishing our new normal.

While I identified as a writer, my writing life was attached to motherhood. I'd spent the past decade writing feature articles and penning monthly columns in numerous mothering and family-centered magazines. Without my youngest child, I was suddenly plunged into an empty nest and into a role for which there was no name—a mother whose child has died.

I was forty-five years old. Friends my age, who were mothers, appeared awkward around me, and some of these friendships grew strained. I saw the fear in their eyes. What every mother feared most had happened to me; I represented their worst nightmare. No doubt some could not bear to think about how awful it would be to bury their own child along with all of their hopes and dreams. I could tell that seeing me shattered, clawing my way back to center, was a horror beyond their worst terror imaginable.

To ease myself into my new identity, I began to seek out friends who were not mothers and had intentionally remained childless. Yet with my running-with-scissors version of motherhood behind me, these friends also appeared to feel uncomfortable around me.

My center of belonging was with Marie, Ann, Irene, and Mary Lou, and it was connected to some of their close friends who were also elders, women I'd come to know from our casual gatherings. With their long-lived lives, each of them had experienced catastrophe, along with multiple deaths. Husbands and children had died. They had evolved through many lifestyle and identity challenges and adjustments, and they were able to relate to me and understand me better than I understood myself.

With Marie, Mary Lou, Ann, Irene, and the elders in writing class, I felt myself growing stronger and weaker. The stronger I became, the more willing I was to allow myself to explore the depth of my sorrow and didn't try to cover up my searing pain. I felt strong enough to let my guard down, exposing how weak I really felt, knowing I wouldn't be swallowed up by darkness. It was necessary to dig deep, and these periods were followed by fallow times, when I let myself absorb what was.

28

PUSHING UP THE SKY

I had begun journaling on a daily basis. Finally, I pulled out the book manuscript for Pushing Up the Sky. It had been sitting in my desk drawer for two years. I began rewriting all of the chapters.

Each week I read a few pages in the Friday morning elders writing group, with Mary Lou sitting next to me. Sometimes when my voice quivered, I could feel the cool skin of her palm cup the back of my neck.

As I read, it felt as if each person in the room had their arms around me. I sniffed my way through each story I read, and when I looked up, I saw many red-rimmed eyes, and the smile on every face put me at ease.

Finally, I finished writing the book.

"Now what do I do?" I said out loud to myself when I had finished writing the book for a second time. But I knew the answer. I needed to write a one-page query letter, a book proposal, and find a publisher.

"I've got the book finished, Bill," I shouted out to the trees.

"And damn it, you have gone off and deserted me. I did my part, and now you are dead and can't keep your end of the bargain."

In my dream that night, I stood in a field of old cars. Bill was there. He asked me to get a putter out of the trunk of his car. I was embarrassed because, of all the golf clubs, I wasn't sure which one was a putter. I stood with the trunk open, peering in.

Bill struggled to get up. I knew he was coming to help me. I wanted his help, but at the same time I felt sorry to be disturbing him because in my dream I understood he was dead.

Before he reached the car, I spotted a manuscript in the trunk. The title was "Putter."

We both looked at the manuscript, and in that moment I knew I had to trust myself. The knowledge was inside me; I already knew what to do, and I needed to listen to myself and do it.

The dream message was not only about writing; it had to do with everything in life.

I must reach with faith, trust myself, and believe.

I began searching for a publisher, and *Pushing Up the Sky: A Mother's Story* was published in 2006.

The title is from a traditional story of the Snohomish tribe, which testifies and speaks to the great power of what we can accomplish when people work together with a common goal.

I wouldn't be here without the steadfast support and love of many people.

After publishing my memoir, sharing my journey through motherhood and the most tender years of my life, I grew quieter than usual, subdued, somber. The book was successful. It was widely anthologized, and I was invited to travel throughout the United States and in South Korea, to sit on panels and give talks. But the book also stirred up controversy, and I had run into some hostility. There are a number of white adoptive parents who are raising their Asian children as white-alike. My story about my kids growing up within our Native community and within our local Korean community was too sharp for some readers, like a new tooth making its way through the gum. I was not prepared for the emotions it stirred in me when my personal life became public.

In 2006, when the book was published, most adoption memoirs were written by white adoptive mothers, and often the books had a Christian slant. There were few motherhood adoption memoirs published by women of color and even fewer published by Native women, and my memoir gained much attention.

I am deeply thankful for the journey provided by the publication of the book. Yet it also meant I continually faced harsh comments.

The "first mother" and "birth mother" community was supportive, and a number of adopted men and women in the transracial adoption community were supportive. But many reader comments from white adoptive mothers only focused on what they thought were my failings. Mainstream readers from outside the adoption triad gave my book good reviews and did not find fault for the way my story unfolded, but I struggled when I received brutal comments from my peer group of adoptive mothers.

I'd lived with so much trauma while growing up and with more trauma again in my adult years. I'd formed a habit of repressing any emotions and memories that caused anyone to become angry. Instead of feeling my emotions and remembering what happened from my point of view, I would revise my memory so that other people would not get angry, or else I just blocked the memory out entirely.

Dealing with negative reader comments and criticism stirred up a myriad of emotions. With little experience feeling my emotions, I went through much anxiety.

Ann had always encouraged me to be open and genuine and to explore my emotions, all of them, and not block out my feelings. She said it wasn't my responsibility to comply with the expectations of other people and that trying to please people or control the angry outbursts of others by suppressing or censoring what I felt or had to say was out of my control.

"The way you feel is your story," Ann said.

"We each have our own story to tell, and you don't need to edit how you feel in order to make it match the expectations of others."

As time went on, more often when feelings and memories blocked up inside me, I was able to let them float back down.

29

GROWING OLD IN A BEAUTIFUL WAY

We were sitting on the beach, soothed by the rhythm of the waves, under a bead-blue sky, an ocean breeze blowing and an occasional hawk sweeping over, with light shining through her rust red tail. I was gathered with Mary Lou, Marie, and Anita, a friend of Marie's who lived in Arizona, near Ship Rock, and she was visiting.

The tang of salt and sea air settled around me. I wiggled my bare toes in the sand and felt the wind and mist from the spray on my hair. Mary Lou sat in her beach chair with her arms and legs relaxed, a flying cloud of white hair spilling out from under her wide-brimmed sun hat. The tide was coming in, and the waves were swelling gently, sheltered by the cove.

Anita slipped off her jeans, pulled off her shirt, and stood facing me, wearing her bathing suit. Her bare skin looked young and old, saggy and supple. A caramel color, with those darker brown spots we develop over the years. I guessed she was about seventy-five. But she may have been much older. The way she stood and carried her body, her neck and shoulders, with a gentle grace was beautiful, and I saw she had a comfortable relationship with her flesh. She lived in her body in a way I didn't.

"I'm going to swim, want to join me?" she asked.

"Yes," I said, surprising myself. I wasn't wearing a bathing suit under my shorts, tank top, and long-sleeve linen shirt. I'm not spontaneous often, and I always regret the fun I miss out on. The day was sunny and warm. I could swim in my shorts, and my tank top would dry. I took off my shirt and walked with Anita toward the surf.

We waded in the water until we were up to our waist and then dove headfirst into the next swell. We let the sea carry us toward shore and then swam out again toward the next swell. I let the sea take over my mind completely. No thoughts, at least not at first. I was one with the circles of the waves, serene.

Back on the beach, with strands of seaweed tangled in my hair, salty with the scent of the ocean, I stretched out on the sand and watched the seagulls dive for fish.

Marie unpacked her homemade tortillas and salsa. Mary Lou pulled out her deviled eggs. I brought out my basket filled with cherry tomatoes and serrano chilies from my garden, and a wide-mouth thermos of beans, fragrant with cumin.

"Is that a Cherokee double-walled basket?" Anita asked.

I nodded. "I don't use it often. It was made by a friend who doesn't follow a pattern. Her pattern ideas come from the shapes of mountains, streams, and forests, and she always makes one crooked stitch with a gap, so spirit can get it."

Anita smiled. "Saving it for good? Be careful. A basket unused and untouched will die. It makes me worry about baskets sitting alone and unused in museums."

Over the years I had woven a number of baskets. I'm unskilled and use only one weaving style, known as the lazy stitch. I thought about how basketry is a concrete expression of Native peoples' seamless connection to the natural world, and I made a plan to begin using my baskets every day, to keep them alive.

It had been a while since we had been together. Checking in, spending a few minutes sharing our thoughts or telling each other what had taken place within our lives, had become our ritual, and it was how we reunited after some weeks apart.

When it was Marie's turn to share, she asked us each to place our hand on our heart. To feel it beating, feel our breath going in and out, to feel the power of our hearts beating within our bodies. Although she was sitting right next to me, her voice sounded far away. The air began pressing down on me, and it was hard to breathe. And that's when I understood I was afraid of my body because instead of power I felt only fear.

I sat with my eyes closed and tried to let my tense muscles relax. Then a terrible panic struck me, and I did not want to continue. I sat frozen, my hand on my heart, thumping wildly, anxiety rising.

I eased the panic as best I could by holding three fingers on the center of my chest, on my breastbone, an acupressure point known as the Sea of Tranquility. I'd studied acupressure when my son had a brain tumor and knew this was a potent point for relieving anxiety and nervousness.

Soon I began to feel calm enough to explore my thoughts. It took me about ten minutes to admit to myself that I was afraid of my body. Afraid of growing old and developing a serious health condition. Afraid that if something did happen to me, it would be all my fault because I ought to be able to take good enough care of my body to prevent anything bad from happening.

I knew this was ridiculous crazy thinking, and yet on some level I believed it. I had grown wise enough to understand that I needed to feel all of my feelings, not just the ones I enjoyed but the uncomfortable ones too. Yet my old habit of running away from uncomfortable emotions still had a hold on me sometimes.

Mary Lou reached over and patted my arm. She was getting smaller as she aged, wrinkling into buttery skin. She held her eyes on mine.

"You will never be able to relax if you are worn-out from worry, swimming against the current of your own life," she said.

I had confided to her, let her know that while I appeared calm, my mind was often a jumbled mix of emotions causing me to feel much anxiety.

I took good care of my body. I fed it healthy foods and took myself for long walks each morning. After my shower I rubbed lotion on my arms and legs, patted moisturizer on my face. I kept my fingernails filed short and smooth, and I painted my toenails and adorned myself with earrings and bracelets. But more often, I worried about my body.

Despite healthy habits and good medical care, I had a growing list of health-related conditions I was managing. And I fretted about my skin. Too much sun had caused irreparable damage. My body was greedy, with a full list of requirements, and I was never willing to be patient with its needs. The ship of myself was not sailing on calm seas.

Yet my favorite woman friends had evolved to another rhythm, able to ebb with years, making adjustment to their individual needs, able to pause and be with difficult times with their bodies. They were moving through the seasons of age without getting tossed away.

Luke once made a comment to me about the way I lived in my mind. He often reminded me to climb back into my body. That afternoon I began seeking out a new design of living, to set myself out on a journey to just *be* inside my body, without judging it. To trust there was beauty within a body growing old, withered and wrinkled.

That day I gained the insight of what it means to be beautiful on the inside and to have that beauty reflect to the outer world. When I felt vulnerable, instead of feeling insecure, I could become curious and see what else I might be feeling and praise myself for sticking around to discover more, instead of running away from the thought. While sitting on the beach, I began to think of uncomfortable feelings as waves, letting them roll in and wash over me, and then I let the thought float out to sea.

I had also become aware that my friends were focusing on what they could do and on what they had, instead of grieving about what was lost or worrying about what might happen next.

Since I spent so much time living in my mind, I began to understand it was necessary for me to create a pattern of thinking positive thoughts. To repeat to myself multiple times each day all of the things I appreciated about my body.

Up until then, I had viewed aging as enchanting—as long as I felt strong and was healthy. I would need to shed my view of health challenges as a period of decline. To learn to view aging as a second flowering, even when my body and my health status were not ideal. This was a big task in a society that makes youthfulness a sign of perfection.

Like many women, I had subscribed to the notion that growing older was inevitable but aging was not. Good looks and good health might be by-products of healthy living. I hoped that they were. But I decided they were no longer my end goals.

My new aim became about the good feelings I gained, in the moment, from my healthy lifestyle each day, without thinking about the future. Luke had lived a lifestyle far healthier than mine, and he didn't live longer than me. But he lived well while he was alive.

I would continue to engage in healthful living and let go of an expected outcome. I'd continue to eat a wide variety of vegetables because I loved vegetables. Black coffee, dark chocolate, good cheese, and good wine would remain, and I'd savor them with joy. I would let go of the guilt. Guilt, I reasoned, would cause harm.

I'd continue walking miles each day because I loved walking.

Never again would I view a healthy lifestyle as a quest for retaining youth.

Once, I was young, with perfect skin and a lovely body, and I used it well. I was still lovely, but I looked different now, and it was my turn to begin experiencing older age.

I wanted to come of age welcoming my changing body, knowing I had enjoyed my body and cared for it as best I could. I'd spent enough years worrying. I would begin to look for ways to enjoy the changes time brought.

Near the end of our day together, I was so relaxed my mind was floating and my thoughts were rolling in and out with the waves. The anxiety I'd felt in the morning was gone. My crystalline revelation of shedding my fear of aging left me feeling like I'd discovered a secret kingdom at the bottom of the sea.

Anita said something reminding me of Auntie.

"Can you please explain a bit more about what you just said?" I asked. "Growing up, my auntie told us stories about women having strong medicine power having to do with their belonging to the feminine powers of the universe. And I've always wondered about it. But when I asked my aunt, she never gave an answer; instead, she just told us another story, the traditional ones, from the oral tradition."

"Shhh," Anita said. "We aren't supposed to talk about it, not unless the powers agree. Otherwise, the powers will turn on you. That's why we tell the medicine stories by teaching the traditional stories."

I felt my face grow hot.

Anita smiled. Her gentle manner put me at ease, and it left me wanting to hear more.

30

WATER CHORES
AND RITUALS

Mary Lou asked me to stop by because she had something to give me.

The sun beamed in from her kitchen window.

She handed me a package tied with ribbons.

I unwrapped a turquoise silk shirt.

"I've only worn it once," she said. "While I was wearing it, I kept thinking of you and how the color would play nice with your green eyes."

We walked together to the mirror. The dark turquoise made my eyes look sea green, like the ocean after a summer rainstorm. I looked up to see Mary Lou blinking at me, smiling. The grooves along her mouth had deepened. Her dimples and rounded cheeks had sunk to hollows.

"Your hair is going gray in a lovely way. Don't color it," she said.

She handed me a picture of a woman with long silver hair, tied back.

"This is me at about your age. I still look the same, in the dark."

She had become so fragile she could not care for herself without help and had decided she would soon move into an assisted living community. Yet her spirit and essence were bright. Her eyes glistened, and a vibrant energy rose from her presence.

"When was the last time you sorted through your closet?" Mary Lou asked.

I shrugged my shoulders.

"Practice wearing only your favorites for a month."

She grinned. "All those lovely things, waiting for a turn to be worn."

On my way out the door that day, Mary Lou clutched my arm and said cheerfully,

"I have friends who come by and offer to help me by doing my laundry, my dishes. But those are the water chores, and I love doing water chores," she explained. "Water chores make me feel alive."

I watched her make her way down the steps, with her cane tucked under her left arm. Stepping slowly, the way I once watched a newborn deer take her first steps. Mary Lou's legs wobbled, but her footing was sure. When she reached the bottom step, she leaned on the rail and planted her right foot on solid ground. Then she leaned forward on her cane and touched my cheek.

"I've been leaving a bowl of water outside on nights when the moon is out and bringing it into my bedroom before I go to bed."

"What?" I asked.

She grabbed my hand. "The other day with Anita at the beach, she told me how moon water could be created by leaving a bowl of clean water outdoors in a place where it would be infiltrated by moonbeams. It can soften the energy in a room, and it works." she whispered.

I walked home and thought about how I also loved doing water chores. Washing the dishes and doing the laundry were peaceful activities, and when I watered the yard, I let the water pool around my feet. Water restored me to calm. I'm sure I have always been this way, but this was the first time I was aware of it. When my writing was blocked and couldn't flow or when my emotions got stuck and I was having a hard time getting them to float back down, I turned to water. Live water was best, the river or the salty ocean or the creek behind my house when it rained, with water rushing over smooth stones.

I called Anita on the telephone to learn more about how water could aid in healing, cleansing, and rejuvenating.

"Oh, Terra!" she said when she answered the phone, "I'm so glad you called me." She said this in her soothing voice that sounded smooth and made me think of her soft caramel skin and easy manner and the way she was comfortable in her body. She spoke slowly, drawing out each word, and the sweet cadence of it let me know she had plenty of time to talk.

"Lunar water, or what we call moon water, can help calm a room, restore the balance, and foster dreaming. To create moon water," Anita explained, "leave a bowl of water outdoors in a place where it will be infiltrated by moonlight. A ceramic or glass bowl is best because the water will also pick up the properties of the type of container used."

She said moon water has a powerful feminine healing aspect and can soften the energy in a room. It is helpful in a room where anger, sadness, and intense emotions have lingered, and it is also good to use in bedrooms to create a peaceful feeling that is helpful for sleep and promotes dreaming.

Anita also said I could make solar, or sun, water by leaving a bowl of water outside in the sunlight for a few hours to soak up the healing properties from the sun. Sun water has an active type energy and is good for dark rooms or room that have a dark or heavy energy. It is also helpful to use in a room where someone has been sick.

Cherokees have water charging rituals, but I don't have much knowledge of this, and I asked Anita if her moon and sun water had a role in her Diné upbringing.

"Oh, goodness no, not in a tribal traditional way. At least I don't think so."

I could tell she was a bit surprised I would think it might be, assuming that I knew better than to think she would talk about Diné rituals in a casual manner with someone she barely knew. I did know better. But I'm also adamant against anything New Agey mixed and made to sound like an American Indian tradition, and not knowing Anita well, ever careful, I had to ask.

"My mom grew up without running water in the house she lived in on her reservation," Anita said. "Gathering water was a way of life. Often pails of water were left outside, overnight sometimes. Or even all day. My mom and her sisters washed their hair and cleaned the house with the left-out water, instead of using fresh water, and they discovered the water left in the daylight or moonlight had different properties, and they figured out that the water energy was different depending on the type of bucket or container used."

She giggled. "Our water ways were not traditional in a tribal way, but it was definitely a major part of my upbringing and something my mother and aunties have much knowledge about and a strong belief in. Since I grew up with much water charging taking place all around me, I've given water more attention than most people do."

After I finished talking with Anita, I got out the small red river rock I'd collected from the shoreline of the river behind Luke's house. Sometimes I carried the rock in the pocket of my jeans. It helped me feel connected to the river and to the landscape.

River rocks change the course of streams and rivers. Many Native people honor river rocks because they contain the energies of the earth and the waters on the earth and are considered to have the medicine of both these elements. River rocks could help with healing, cleansing, stabilizing, or changing your life, and working with them could release negative patterns, especially emotional ones.

Then an idea came to me. I put the river rock in the bathtub and filled the tub with water, and I climbed in. I could almost smell the piñon and sage that blew in the wind across the backbone of the ridge above the river. My mind floated back over time, to the day when I walked barefoot along the riverbank and picked up the rock. The red clay soil was slippery, and it stuck to the soles of my feet. Then I waded knee-deep into the river. It was the day the lizard sat in my lap.

My mind rolled back, and I remembered how I hadn't wanted to take a bath before I went to bed that night when I was staying at Luke's place. The river water had soaked into my skin. I felt calm. It was a feeling of knowing I did not want to wash off the river.

I ran more hot water in the tub and soaked with the river rock for a long time. When I climbed out, I went straight to bed and drifted into a deep, peaceful sleep.

31

THE LANDSCAPE WILL
TEACH YOU WHO YOU ARE

Two days later I was planning to wear the silk shirt Mary Lou gave me, but when I looked out the window, I saw smoke and flames in the mountains above our house. It was a warm, windy day, with low humidity, and the fire was traveling fast.

We evacuated to a friend's home near the ocean. I centered down with my community, again. Two fires within the past year. Homes burned, and lives lost. Fifteen catastrophic fires within the past twenty-five years. I could hear the ancestors telling me it will happen again and again. When we build our cities, homes, near these foothills, we cannot expect permanency, on this coastal mountain range, in this land of drought. Fire is a story waiting.

We lived in a canyon area below the foothills in a high fire danger area. We've had a number of fires over the years that burned deep into our neighborhood. So far, we have been lucky, and our home was spared.

There was a part of me that wanted to move away, but we lived in a wonderful place when fire was not present. And there was a greater part of me that wanted to let go of my attachment to things. To enjoy what I had, to deepen my spiritual understanding with an awareness and mindset that if it was lost, it wouldn't be the end of me.

I wanted to believe I'd be sad, deeply sad, but that I would rise again.

I've lived side by side with neighbors and close friends whose homes did burn, and they rebuilt their houses and their lives. When I stood beside them, I never imaged myself as being that strong.

The first time we had to evacuate with a fire looming nearby, we were given about an hour's notice. I had three young children at the time, and my first and only thought was to get them safely in the car. We gathered the dog and cat next, and then the police came to tell us not to leave yet, to wait until they came for us because they were escorting families out since the roadway was jammed with traffic. Gary sat in the car with the kids and suggested I run and grab a few necessities for the children and get some of our "special" things. But when I went back into our house, what we had previously viewed as special looked unimportant.

What should I save? It was in the days before digital photography, so I grabbed the photo albums. Next, I walked from room to room, surveying our belongings. I had a nice house filled with lovely things, but all of my prized possessions looked like junk. In that moment I understood that what I appreciated most was the washing machine, our beds, the bathtub, the refrigerator. And our kitchen, where hours earlier I was happily preparing lunch, unaware that by dinnertime we would be in danger of losing our home and possibly our lives.

With each fire and forced evacuation, I always managed to see the upside, but I also began to gain a sense of urgency and went into a deep, primal, hunting and gathering, survival mode. It came from having to leave the dinner on the table one evening when flames were spotted nearby and from having to comfort hungry children throughout the night. Four years later, when the next fire occurred, I evacuated with food supplies.

The drought in California was severe again, and once again, we were facing extremely high fire danger. Yet I'd begun to feel something settle down inside me. There was a quiet calm born of knowing I no longer thought of my possessions as an extension of myself.

I was moderately minimalistic in most aspects of my life. We lived a casual lifestyle, grew a garden, and we liked to cook. The car I drove was an older economy model. My home was decorated in an economical simple style; it was comfortable and inviting, and it was clutter free. I thought of myself as a down-to-earth, sensible person. But my closet told another story.

Although I frequently purchased items on sale and never had any credit card debt, after being brought into a circle of woman who placed value on friendship and community belonging more than possessions, it occurred to me that I had too many clothes, and I was spending too much money and squandering my time shopping for unnecessary clothes. And like many people, I saved my favorite things for good.

I thought about Mary Lou's advice to only wear my favorites.

I also thought about what I'd learned from Anita, about baskets needing to be used or else they would die. Every material thing is made up of energy, including clothing, and this energy needs to be touched and used, moved about, and not allowed to become stagnant. The clothes I seldom wore, or never wore at all, just sat in the closet year after year.

It felt like my closet had begun to communicate with me. It was speaking, letting me know the airflow was trapped and that everything needed to be moved out, touched, held, and used so the energy could move around.

I sorted through my closet and found lots of good clothes, more clothes than I needed or had opportunities to wear. As I pulled out my favorites, my eyes crinkled in happy satisfaction. I rifled through my collection of business wear and made the decision to give away many nice outfits suitable for working in an office and donated them to a charity that gave clothing to women in the workforce who were in need.

My lifestyle had grown casual. I was working in an informal environment, providing me with the freedom to wear casual skirts and jeans. Most of all I'd changed and no longer wanted or felt the need to have an excessive amount of clothing.

I stopped buying too many clothes and began wearing my favorite things on a regular basis and discovered having a small wardrobe of clothing I enjoyed wearing regularly was more fun.

I called Mary Lou.

"I've given up the habit of saving things for special occasions."

"Good job. An A+," she said.

Once I had tamed my closet and rid myself of excess, I began to examine and reevaluate my shopping habits and my consumptive nature in other areas of my life.

The changes I made brought me back to caring deeply about sustainability and interconnectedness, traditional Native values I was raised with but which were slipping away from me.

While I will never be a minimalist in a sense of wanting to live with as little as possible, I've come to understand that I enjoy the minimalist lifestyle of owning less. It provided me with freedom, calm, and gave me greater satisfaction than owning an abundance of things ever did.

I also began to understand living with the threat of fire for many years had taught me valuable life skills and good habits. We kept the dog leash by the front door. The cat carrier was in an easy-to-reach location. I was careful to keep my car keys, cell phone, charger, my glasses, and my purse organized and within easy reach. Gone were the days when I plunked things down without thinking about where I'd put them.

There is an "idea" that when fire threatens, and given ample time and if safety permits, a person will want to save the valuables. But in my neck of the city-woods, we had learned that what's most valuable when you must evacuate your home is a pair of jeans, shoes, a jacket, a blanket—and a car that is not stuffed to the roof with useless belongings. Because chances are you will need to sleep in that car, along with the kids, the dog, and the cat.

From multiple times of needing to leave quickly to evacuate, the lesson my family members, neighbors, and I have learned is that when your closet (or your entire house) is jam-packed, it is impossible to pull out a few necessary key items quickly.

And if you are given the luxury of time and safety, having fewer belongings makes it much easier to find and grab what you need and run out the door.

I never imagined I would grow to view fire as a wise teacher and embrace her lessons. Yet each time I cleaned and decluttered my home, my motto was, if I was not using an item, then it was better to give it to someone who would. Because I wouldn't have a second chance to give it away if the fire took it.

I also began thinking about the right use of world resources, and the exploitation of garment workers and manufacturing workers called me to reflect deeply.

Before purchasing or acquiring anything, I began the habit of asking myself:

How much do I actually need it, in comparison to what it has taken from the planet and from workers and from others in order to produce it?

How often will I use it, and how long will it last? When and how will I dispose of it?

I know for sure, though, you don't have to experience a fire to learn the value of deciding to live with less. Yet for me living with fire had become a lens through which to examine my own life.

32

SAFEKEEPING

My changing mentality of material possessions has been a strong theme in my life for as long as I can remember. When my thoughts roll back to my childhood home, the bottom drawer, at the end of the long hallway, near my bedroom, stands center in my mind.

There were four drawers, with four shelves above. The shelves contained towels, sheets, and blankets. I can't recall what the drawers held; I can only remember the summer day I rearranged whatever was in there and claimed the bottom drawer for my own use. I was twelve years old.

It was a wide, deep drawer. I unpacked the shoebox where I kept my special things. Letters and postcards from friends, ticket stubs, photos, sandalwood incense, a peace sign neckless and hippie beads made by a friend. Feathers, small rocks, and natural stones, my diary, the book I wrote in a spiral tablet when I was ten years old. I moved all of it into the bottom drawer.

I don't remember my mother saying anything to me about taking over the drawer. What I do remember is how full that drawer had become by the time I was seventeen and the late nights I sat on the floor, sorting through the drawer, revisiting my past, wandering back over time.

A ticket stub from a Rolling Stones concert I had carried in my coat pocket for weeks reminded me of the night my friend Jerry came over, and my friend Sherry was with him. Luke came over that night too. That night I put on my coat, we went for a drive, then hiked up to Houdini's Castle in the Hollywood Hills. The caretaker's hot-breathed dogs met us ten feet from the mansion, snarling. Luke grabbed my hand, we ran fast, my fingernails gripping into his palm. The night at the castle reminded me of the time Jerry and I ditched high school to go skiing, but we got in a car wreck, rolled his vw. It was our senior year in high school. Almost getting killed together gave us a sturdy bond. I remembered how in friendship I was kind of hoping he would ask me to the senior prom. He didn't; he asked my friend Peggy.

The photo of Luke, the one he gave me after we turned our relationship into just friends. A red ribbon I won in a relay race when we lived in Compton was somehow connected to my memories of wanting to take diving lessons. When it came to swimming and diving, I was becoming a good diver off the high dive, better than average.

My uncle's enrollment card, documenting his tribal citizenship. He gave it to me one Sunday afternoon and asked me to keep it for a while, to remind myself who I am. Afraid of losing it, I kept it in a small jewelry box inside my special drawer.

When I opened that drawer, my heart blared open, and time stopped around me, like a scene held in a snowy globe.

My final memory of the drawer is the night it was so heavy I almost could not pull it out. On my knees, leaning forward, I lifted, strained, and rocked it gently until it began to slide. When it came out halfway, all at once the bottom of the drawer fell out, spilling the contents, and the wood frame splintered.

The moment the drawer broke, along with the panic I felt, I remember feeling a sense of freedom and peace. I had saved so much stuff, and it had become a burden, both physically and emotionally. In that moment I understood I was ready to let some of it go.

I was also worried about how my dad would react to the broken drawer. I couldn't fix it by myself. I would need to ask for his help.

But my dad wasn't angry. He just fixed the drawer.

The next day I culled my collections and tossed out what I no longer wanted to keep. The release came on easy, with a feeling of knowing it was time and I was ready to shed some layers of stuff. I filled many brown paper bags and tossed them in the trash, and I placed the things I still wanted to keep in a strong cardboard box and put it in my closet, on the floor.

After I moved my stuff out and my dad fixed the drawer my awareness shifted. I began to develop some kind of deep understanding that what I had amassed fell into two categories. The things that belonged to versions of myself based on what my interests were at various stages in my life and in that moment in time. And the tender things that were infused with memories and emotions I wanted to hold onto or had not yet dared to fully explore. Love, pain, and grief.

I saved some of my keepsakes for years and then began to understand when something had served its purpose. I had loved it, and it had played an important role, and now I was done.

I kept that box of saved things for decades. It was a good, strong box with a lid. In time I stopped putting in new treasures, but I saved some of the old stuff for years. Each time I moved, I carried that box with me from house to house.

Then came the day when I peered inside at the contents and became aware of what was not inside my box of treasures, what couldn't be seen and can't be packed up. It was the memories tucked into the margins of my mind, floating on air currents, of the events that have shaped me into the woman I am today.

Once again, I explored the contents of the box. Again, I culled, and this time I tossed out the cardboard box and placed some of the small things I wanted to keep inside a little black walnut box made by a friend.

This wooden box links me back in time. It carries me to the day my friend showed me the wooden boxes he was making, to the moment I admired his work, and the morning he showed up early at my house and gave me the box.

When I open the box, it takes me back to the drawer in my childhood hallway. I can smell the night-blooming jasmine from my open bedroom window, see blue dark of night with a passing car reflecting the corner streetlight outside. I can feel my teenaged self, sitting on the hallway floor.

My mind can see the opened drawer filled with certificates, awards, funny photographs, letters saved from a friend in the navy, stationed in Japan, his careful script written on parchment paper. Letters from a boy named Donny, bundled together and tied with a hot pink rope of yarn. All of it comes back to me, the same as if I were opening the drawer right now.

I was discovering that memory waves rolled through me and were frequently triggered by scents; the fragrance woke up my emotions.

When I sliced lemons or when the air was heavy with the salty ocean, I was returned to the mornings when my bare feet poked into a tangle of blue morning glory and sunbaked lemon rinds, with the scent of mulch and sea air settling around me, and I remembered and felt myself sitting on a bench under the oak tree, near the compost pit. This was my favorite getaway spot when I was in my early twenties. It was a quiet place to be alone with my thoughts.

When I moved to another house, I dug a new compost pit. Next to the compost pit, I leveled the ground and made a place for the trash barrel to sit. Long ago, to the trash I sent an old favorite *Peter, Paul, and Mary* record, along with a note from Luke written on the inside flap. Music came to me in the form of iTunes. All of my favorite *Peter, Paul, and Mary* albums were on my playlist. I no longer owned a turntable, the record was badly warped, and while cleaning out the closet one Saturday morning, I sent my beloved to the trash.

I held the cardboard album cover close to my chest, hugged myself, and let thirty years of memories run through me. Golden sunlight fell on my shoulders and heated up my dark-blue flannel shirt. Gently, I tossed the record into the trash.

Sometimes, when I least expected it, when I took out the trash, I smelled the scent of sour lemon rinds rotting, the sharpness of decomposed grass, and I remembered all those late nights we listened to *Peter, Paul, and Mary* records and all of the *Peter, Paul, and Mary* concerts I went to with Luke.

I believe a pattern developed the night my drawer broke. When deciding what to save, I weighed the memories I had associated with the objects. What memory was I trying to hold onto? How much grief did I feel? What kind of pain? What kind of love?

When I tossed out the album, I was tossing away the pain I felt in my teenage years. The terrible grief I felt growing up in a home with yelling, screaming, crying, hitting, and the threats. The opportunities lost. Roads not taken. The way I felt lost in a maze.

Yet somehow letting go of the record also unlocked love. In order to toss out pain, I was also tossing out love. My stomach unclenched; the knots in my shoulders gave up their grip on me. I remembered how in those late nights, listening to music, I felt tender, sheltered, secure. My heart was wide open, lying on the floor on our backs, with the volume turned up loud early in the evening and then turned down low, with our ears near the speaker, when the night grew late. On those nights I let myself feel safe, happy, loved. Then in the morning I sealed myself back up.

I began to understand that since I was deficient when it came to my feelings and I didn't show my emotions, I saved things instead. Later, when I felt ready, I could hold the object in my hand and pay attention to how my body responded. Did my stomach feel tight? Was I holding my breath? When I could not name the emotion surging, I could feel it in my body.

Figuring out that scents unlocked my memories—and my emotions—was a powerful discovery. It made it easier not to save everything. I was noticing that in my mind, whatever I'd let go of was still there, I still had it, just not in the physical sense.

I was finding my rhythm, becoming in tune with my growing and changing self. Getting comfortable with allowing myself to evolve and willing to let go of what I'd collected in each phase from my past self but had outgrown the need to save in order to let myself move on.

Still, there was one category of material belongings that had a strong hold on me. It was my clothing. I grew up poor but not in poverty. My grandmother sewed wonderful dresses for me, but I only had a handful of dresses at a time, probably just enough for me to have a week's worth of clean dresses to wear to school each day, and yet I never felt

I was lacking. I always felt that the clothes I had looked great on me, and I was content. I felt secure, confident.

My early adult years were not focused on an overabundance of clothes, and then somewhere along the way I took a wrong turn.

With Mary Lou urging me on, I'd reduced the amount of clothing I had to a manageable number of outfits. It felt good to be returned to my roots. A homecoming. Coming back to my core values, gained within a culture and lifestyle back in a time, when the average amount of clothing a woman owned was far less than what is considered average today.

I felt good about giving away the things I no longer wanted to wear or save. I wasn't overly attached to any of the clothes I no longer wanted to wear. But I did have an extreme attachment and a great fondness for the memories attached to my clothes. The clothes of my life are a scrapbook in my mind. The brown suede coat I saved up for when I was sixteen. Months of saving. The day I wore the coat out of the store, breathing in the scent of new leather, and how the suede was an exact match with my long brown hair.

The hot-pink velvet A-line dress my grandmother made for me when I was thirteen. Standing on a footstool in her bedroom so that she could get the hemline short enough. The prick of straight pins poking into my bare skin and my grandmother's soft hands, smoothing over my thigh, easing the spot where the pins had poked me.

When I was fourteen, baby doll dresses were on every girl's wish list. The one my grandmother made for me had a white eyelet bodice, with puff sleeves, and the attached skirt was a gold gingham. It was the summer between eighth and ninth grade, when my legs were tanned dark and slathered with Coppertone lotion.

The year I was a senior in high school, Grandma and I searched the discount fabric stores. For the homecoming dance, I picked a russet velvet. The dress she made for me was floor-length, with long sleeves, an empire waist, and a plunging deep V-neckline. We used the same pattern for my prom dress, with yards of turquoise satin. This time I asked Grandma to make the neckline a bit deeper.

When I think about the places I've been, the things I've done, sad or happy memories, most of the time I can remember what I was wearing. I can see and feel the fabric in my mind, the colors, the patterns, textures. I remember if it was comfortable or if it itched.

For me clothing and jewelry are wearable art. Pure joy and fun. But I'm a causal dresser. I don't like to dress up, unless the occasion requires it. I'm happiest wearing jeans, sandals, and cotton or linen shirts, with Native-made earrings, silver, beaded or natural stone.

As attached as I've always been to my clothes, when I was young, it never bothered me when I outgrew something I loved and it was handed down to a younger cousin because I could count on having new clothes each year in a bigger size.

I'm still happy to give away anything I'm not using. But I have deep affection and an attachment to the clothes I'm currently wearing at any given point in time.

I do not check my luggage on air flights. I'm content bringing only a few things in a small soft-sided carry-on bag, and I'm an outfit repeater. If I love something, I will wear it twice a week.

In one of my favorite memoirs, the author wrote about a family tragedy that required her to catch a flight home as soon as possible. She said, "While I was taking a shower, my husband packed my bag for me." I wondered what it might be like to be that girl. To be content wearing whatever he packed in her suitcase.

Years ago, I read a book, fiction, in which the author used one perfect sentence to reveal character: "She was the only girl I've ever known who could fit all of her clothes in two dresser drawers." I wondered what it might be like to be that girl too.

Instead, I was the woman who had lost her way and, without any prior history of over-shopping, had amassed more clothes than she could ever wear in any given month.

For the longest time I had no idea what had caused me to go overboard with clothes.

I didn't know why, and it didn't matter; with Mary Lou's help, I had found my way back.

Then, all at once, I understood. I felt lost after my grandparents died. First, my grandfather walked on, and the banjo and mandolin songs he loved best played in my mind.

A year later my grandmother died, and I spent the first years after her death buying clothes, trying to hold onto her.

33

READING, LIVING, AND MY BOOKS

I was a former clothes horse and packrat, with overstuffed closets, and I was becoming a woman who thrived with less. I had begun to edit all of my belongings, and now my beloved things and household possessions and clothing were narrowed down to only the things I loved and that were beautiful, useful, and necessary.

Our home wasn't bare. It still contained many things. We had baskets, artwork, color, flowers, music, and fun dishes to serve the food we prepared. I had sentimental items from my children, husband, and friends. I had begun to figure out that my favorite keepsakes were things I frequently used. The pair of turquoise and spiny oyster shell earrings I gushed over but would not buy. "Too expensive!" I whispered.

When we got into the car, Gary handed me the earrings. For twenty-five years I've enjoyed wearing those earrings. The silver bracelets I never take off. Gary and I searched for a long time until we found the Navajo silver artist who made a style of bracelet to fit my small wrist. The tiny beaded medicine pouch Ann made for me years ago, which I wore all the time.

When I made beans the way Glenda always had or made salsa following Marie's recipe. Watching my son's favorite movies and the bowl of round smooth stones we collected together that now sat in a basket on my coffee table. The thousand paper cranes.

I still had plenty of stuff. Especially books. My bookshelves were filled.

When a close friend, who was my age, was nearing the end of life, after living for a long time with cancer, she invited all of her friends to come browse her bookshelves and to take home some of her books. I loved this gesture and wanted to do the same thing if I was lucky enough to know ahead of time, before my death day arrived.

The books in my home showed a trail of my life. I had books filled with my own writings, the writings of friends, and other authors' work. Memories of afternoons in used bookstores. Portions of my life spent at Tattered Cover Bookstore in Denver. Green Apple Books in San Francisco. Earthling and Chaucer's in Santa Barbara. Bookshop Santa Cruz.

Words offered in countless readings. The weekly bookstore date ritual my son and I had while he was growing up. Books purchased in airports during long flight delays. The year I threw myself a birthday party and asked my friends to bring me a used book they had loved.

Each time I cleaned and organized and made piles of things to release from my life, my books remained untouched. And then everything changed, when days later I was still thinking about what Mary Lou said.

She said, "I should have completed the job of downsizing when I was stronger and my health was better." She was in the process of moving out of the home she had lived in for many years, into assisted living, and was deciding what to keep.

Then she said, "Have you ever thought about what you are going to do with your stuff when you do not have the strength to take care of it?"

I thought about Bill and his yard sale, when he sold a majority of his belongings before moving into a small apartment. That day, when I was helping Bill sell his things, the emotions I felt overwhelmed me, and I had to keep blocking out what I was feeling in order to get the job done. Yet over the years since I never stopped thinking about it. When I smelled fresh-cut grass or unfolded a blue plastic tarp to go camping, the scent unlocked memories, and I was returned to that day at Bill's house, with the yard sale in progress, standing in his driveway, feeling a well of emotions now of what I could not feel then.

Gary and I planned to move into a much smaller space within the next year or two. We no longer wanted to carry the expense and upkeep of the family-sized house we had raised our kids in.

I walked through my house taking stock of all of the heavy things I planned to give away before we moved to a smaller home and before my back grew weak. Already I had begun having problems with my back.

It came down to one thing. My back was strong enough in the moment, and my hardcover books were heavy. I made phone calls and made lists, and I boxed up a goodly number of my books and carted them off to my favorite used book charity sale. I kept only the books I still had not read or books that I kept returning to year after year.

For me the characters in my favorite books are my friends. Relationships I think about long after I finish reading the book. My most loved books left me feeling the author had invited me over for a long chat at her kitchen table. I favored memoirs so intimate I felt myself leaning over the shoulder of the writer, feeling her thoughts and sneaking into her life.

But I no longer needed to keep all of the books I've loved because the memory of the way those stories made me feel had been carved into my heart.

34

THE WINTER MY
GRANDFATHER APOLOGIZED

With my mind centered on how the stories in books left me feeling, my thoughts veered to how some of the people in my life left me feeling. My mom and dad had been divorced for more than fifty years, and my father's angry edge had softened. Between visits we developed a pattern of talking on the telephone. We fell into a comfortable rhythm, with me asking questions, and he began sharing stories about his great-grandmother. He had grown up with her, and he was filling in the details for me, giving shape and color to the stories my own great-grandmother had left out when she talked about her mother.

Long ago I gave up any hope of being able to connect with my dad's father, and my relationship with this grandfather had grown distant. He was doing his best to pass as white, turning his back on his own people, and I refused to follow his lead. Whenever he was around, I put up with him, more or less, until the day he phoned saying he wanted to talk with me.

We sat on the couch, side by side. My grandfather's brown ankles were thin inside his woolen house shoes. His voice was low, barely above a whisper.

"I know I've put a lot of pressure on you to pass as white, and I'm sorry about that. It wasn't the right thing to do."

I was so startled by his admission, my hands were trembling.

"With your light skin, I thought if you could forget about being

Indian, it would make your life easier. But now I can see that by pushing you to forget, it just made things harder for you."

For the first time my grandfather told me about his life, what it was like for him to be an Indian boy, a teenager, a young man. How hard his life had been, the discrimination he faced. He told me about the years when they were sharecroppers. About how Indians didn't sharecrop and the shame he felt. But they had no other way to survive. He talked about how poor they were. How they didn't have a solid roof on some of the shacks they called home, only tarps to keep out the rain, snow, cold, and wind. And about how hard he worked to better his life, finally deciding to ride the rails in train boxcars to get to California. When he arrived, he wanted to leave being Indian behind him. Now he was embracing everything he had run from.

We sat together, side by side, and while he told me his stories, I saw the world through my grandfather's eyes, lived his life, and felt his emotions.

Next, he told me about what it was like for Auntie. She was two years younger than him, with darker skin, deep-set small dark eyes, crow-black hair reaching past her waist, and a shapely figure, curvy in the right places.

"Lydia [Auntie] had it real rough. White men gave her a hard time. We had to watch out for her. Being an Indian girl, those men didn't think she had a right to tell them no."

Grandpa's voice grew a little bit louder, and he told me about a sign a few miles outside of town, before the turnoff onto the dirt road leading to his childhood home in the early 1900s.

The sign said, WHITE MAN DON'T LET THE SUN GO DOWN.

My grandfather looked at me and cleared his throat. "It meant if you were white, then you'd better leave before dark."

There was a sparkle in his eyes. "Back then we could follow a sunset for miles, and most of the time we never met up with anyone or any trouble."

I'd just returned from visiting family in Oklahoma, and I rattled off questions, feeling like a ten-year-old kid again, and this time that deep empty space inside me began to fill up.

35

RIVER IN THE BLOOD

The day after my grandfather apologized, I went to my uncle.

"When I was little, I remembered living near the Mississippi," I confided. "But now all I can remember is the wagons and the tall grass."

Uncle, with his long gray hair feathering behind his ears, peered at me over the rim of his glasses. I watched his face, searching for his thoughts.

"My mom said it must have been a dream because I was born and raised in California."

We were sitting outside, and it was growing dark. Uncle struck a match and lit the lantern. Our night shadows danced against the smooth silver wall of his trailer house. I saw my reflection in the window, the profile of my nose and the way the bones above my cheeks jutted out and formed little mountains below my eyes, curving gently to my jawline. And the way the white hairs streaking through my brown hair danced in the night breeze.

Uncle stared at me for a long time before he spoke.

"Your great-great-grandparents made their home along the river. They lived there in flooding years and in drought years, when the Mississippi was a thin stream in a dry bed, and they lived by that river in times of plenty, pulling their dinner from the water."

"That river is in your blood."

Then Uncle closed his eyes and said, "There is a kind of power sent for knowing, for feeling, and for telling the stories."

His eyes stayed closed, and I wondered if his mind had gone to where the medicine people go, to a space where this world parts so the other can begin.

It's a place I can't find. Yet when I write stories about the time when buffalo grass and red dirt covered the Great Plains between Kansas and the Red River, I know I'm getting close.

36

BACK IN THOSE DAYS IN OKLAHOMA

Glenda had moved back to Oklahoma. It was the last time I saw her after a long stretch. She was living on Kiowa land in Lawton. The land smelled like fast horses and sweet dirt, with something always brewing behind the clouds. Silence replaced noise.

The day I arrived, her tree was raining cherries. Sweet cherries do not thrive in Oklahoma, but sour cherries do. Glenda had picked all morning, filling gallon buckets, and her hands were stained as red as Lady Macbeth's. I helped her deliver some to neighbors, and she put a gallon in the freezer.

We spent the weekend taking long walks and catching up with each other's lives and recollecting old times.

On the last day of our visit, she unwrapped a small package folded in white tissue paper. Inside were the beaded earrings I'd admired many years ago. The ones with a heartbreaking quality of lightness in the way the strands of turquoise beads reflected light. She handed them to me.

"A dear friend made them. She died about a year ago, and they truly are the only thing I have of hers, and I want you to have them."

I blinked for a moment and stared at her, and then I put on the earrings. For a moment everything went silent. The present melted into the past. I remembered when Glenda had long hair, shiny black, and when she tossed it back, it fell over her shoulders like a shawl. Now her hair was the color of smoke, cut short, and when she laughed, her pouty lips and crooked tooth made her look like Joan Baez. Aged into beauty.

A few months later my mother received word that Glenda had died.

When I think of my last day with her, I remember the sun setting with both of us talking fast, trading stories. Laughing together in the gathering twilight and the sky turning indigo, with a warm breeze carrying the sweet fragrance of a distant storm, and then I walked silently out of her house, wearing her earrings.

37

MY MOTHER

Two weeks after I turned sixty-eight, my mother turned eighty-four. We celebrated our birthdays together. It was a mild-mannered, family-centered gathering. My mother had calmed down. Her party days were over. She had become the regular mother I had always wanted her to be. She made casseroles for dinner, read or watched television, and was in bed by midnight.

My mom had gone back to school, got her high school diploma, earned a college degree, and had worked full-time as a children's library assistant.

She still had that special something all of her friends loved and admired. When other people who knew both of us, but didn't know we were related, realized that she was my mom, their eyes sparkled, and they said with fondness and love, "Oh, she is your mom!" My heart filled with pride that she was loved by so many people. Looking back, I'm glad my mom had the opportunity to reclaim her lost teenage years when I was a teenager. But I didn't always like it while I was growing up.

Still, things needed to play out the way they did in order for me to be who I am now, and I like where I have landed. And my mother was my biggest cheerleader. When I shared details of my writing and publishing life with my mom, she was always eager to hear my stories and responded with maternal advocacy.

After my mom retired and had more free time. She slid her glasses down her nose and smiled at me. "Now I can catch up on reading some of your published essays. I think there are some out there that I've missed."

38

ANN, WILMA, JOY, AND ME

I woke up earlier than usual, and while I sat on the porch drinking my coffee, I watched a red-tailed hawk circle up from the bottom of the canyon and glide past, wings spread wide to catch the wind. Then a second hawk glided past, and then a third arrived in the air and was joined by a fourth.

Then I drove over to Ann's house. She wanted to teach me how to make tule dolls so that I could assist her with a craft class she was leading for children. Many California Indian tribes make tule dolls, and each tribe has its own traditional style. The majority of the kids in her class were Chumash, and we were making Chumash fashioned tule dolls. Ann had a large tub of tule reeds that had been soaking in water overnight. First, before I could begin learning, the reeds needed to be cut into specific lengths and organized into groups. For each doll we would need to cut two pieces, sixteen inches long, and eight to fourteen pieces cut into eight-inch lengths. The table we worked on was wet from the soaked reeds, and I pushed up my sleeves.

Ann showed me how to flatten the wet tule reed, then to fold the long piece in half, center a second short tule over the folded one, and fold both halves over. Ann continued showing me how to flatten the tule reeds and how to fold. When she was satisfied with my progress, she handed me a towel to dry my hands and planted herself on a tall kitchen stool.

Ann glanced at me. "Joy Harjo will be at the Native student center. Everybody is going to be there. Are you coming?" she asked.

The following week I went with Ann to the university in our town, to the Native Student Center, a place I frequent. All afternoon, with Joy as our guest of honor, we exchanged laughter, relaxed conversation, prayer, and held ceremony together outside on the grass, with the trees and birds. Later that evening we all had dinner together, and Joy played her music for us. She read to us. The student lounge was filled with Native people from our community—Native students, parents, teachers, and the elders—and I was comforted with our common Indigenous bond, our shared essence, with the jokes that didn't need explaining. It was a good day to be alive.

At the end of that beautiful evening, while we were walking back to the car, Ann and I began reminiscing, recalling another treasured day long ago at the Native Student Center, when we met Wilma Mankiller, former principal chief of the Cherokee Nation. We spent an entire day with Wilma, gathered with other Native women in our community.

Like Marie and Mary Lou, Wilma had a way of letting you know that there wasn't any place in the world she would rather be than with you in the moment. I had only just met her, and yet within a couple of hours, she made me feel like we were longtime friends with the way she leaned close and listened. The thoughtful way she responded. The silence we shared, and then a few minutes later, she picked back up with the conversation, after taking time to consider.

It was the day I began to realize that I don't listen well. I'm too busy worrying about keeping up with the conversation and thinking about what I might say next. Not because I want the attention on me. I don't want to be center stage. My insecurity causes me to fail at listening.

With Wilma I felt secure, safe, and I listened, really listened, for the first time ever.

39

MY RELATIONSHIP
WITH HONESTY

"If you are avoiding something, it's important." Marie looked at me, then she looked down at the brown paper bag I had filled with avocados. She grinned at me, and her dimples deepened into the smile lines mapping her face.

Our avocado tree was loaded; the stems had turned woody. It was time for picking, and I'd invited a few friends to come by and get avocados.

After I filled a bag for Marie, we sat down at the pine table in my kitchen, facing southeast, toward the creek. Outside it was a sunny, hot day. Our view was of the terra-cotta birdbath, with two thirsty scrub jays taking turns drinking and splashing. Behind the birdbath in my backyard, my dog was rooting around. She had developed a taste for avocados.

We were chatting, and I don't recall what we were talking about, only that all of a sudden Marie said: "If you are avoiding something, it's important. Pay attention to anything you don't want to deal with."

I watched the sunlight glinting off the water in the birdbath and the space where the leaves under the avocado tree blended from mud to grass.

"Clear a path in your mind and let go of the thoughts holding you back and make space for spirit to get in." Marie leaned forward, and her dark eyes searched my face.

I tensed my shoulders and tightened my toes. After that brief conversation, I spent a few miserable days feeling uncomfortable, mulling over all of the things I was trying to avoid. Then I got to thinking about my relationship with honesty.

With other people I was accountable, but I did not feel that same sense of accountability with myself. Frequently, I lied to myself. Too often I promised myself I would not do something, and then later I would go ahead and do it anyway.

Maybe the standards I set for myself were too high. I never held others to the standards I aspired to. I did not judge others. I didn't have time. I was too busy judging myself. More often I was trying to fix myself. Often telling myself "No" or "Don't" and not looking past my imperfections long enough to see all of the good things about myself.

I also avoided exploring emotions that made me feel uncomfortable by telling myself they were not important or that they didn't matter, and this was the most insidious way I lied to myself.

It began as a survival tactic. I'd met with too many people who were quick to anger, held grudges, and became hostile and defensive, and I learned to steer. My natural tendency was to be candid, forthright, and passionate. As a child, I knew myself to be too sassy. I talked back and was frequently slapped.

In the slice of America where I'm from, being slapped, spanked, and whipped was commonplace in the 1950s. I can't remember when my parents stopped trying to punish me this way. Maybe it ended when I was around eight or nine, after I figured out how to keep it from happening.

When I was young, I was angry about the face slapping and whippings both of my parents delivered. And I never blocked out my anger. I let it run through me, white-hot and molten, and worked it out of my system by slugging the tetherball, running, swimming.

When I came out on the other side, their behavior served as a guide.

By the time I was in my teens, I'd discovered it could be downright dangerous to talk back or express any emotion that might cause some people to overreact. In middle school a girl slammed me against the lockers, slapping me around, because she "thought" I said something about her that she didn't like. Fortunately, I'd had plenty of experience with people who went off, and I knew how to calm her.

After that episode I learned to watched for clues. When I talked freely and spoke my mind, if I saw a certain look in a person's eyes, suggesting I might get hit or be verbally bashed, I backed off and talked them down.

Learning to control what I said and avoid being hit was easy compared to finding ways to avoid being verbally slammed. My parents seldom struck me with words. The verbal slashings I encountered came later in life. They could pop up anywhere. At school, at work, within white society and within Indian Country, they could happen anyplace, and this served as another training ground to keep my emotions in check as much as possible.

I discovered it was best with some people if I only expressed happy emotions. My mother and my husband fell into this category. Their personalities were similar in the manner in which it caused much discord when I disagreed with them. My mother became deeply hurt and defensive, until I was able to convince her that I was only a little bit annoyed. My husband was harder to manage. He became defensive and lashed out and did not give me a second chance, no opportunity to redeem myself.

It didn't make sense to me, and I could not understand their behavior. Both my mother and my husband were too opinionated and bossy at times, making it necessary for me to disagree with them, and they reacted as if it were all my fault.

The message I received was clear. There must be something wrong with me. Something I needed to fix. Avoid showing strong emotions or censor my thoughts and feelings before speaking or don't say anything at all. Not just with my mother and my husband—I watched other people react this way to each other too. Friends I barely knew and didn't want to know better and coworkers seemed to be equally caught up in it. But they appeared to revel in discord. They wore their anger and hostility like a badge. They accepted it as normal, and I could not.

My remedy for solving this problem was to suppress my emotions. Suppressing my emotions made it hard for me to reach out. When this happened, I told myself I didn't care. But I did care. I cared a lot. I watched other people respond easily and express and show their emotions. It came natural for them. Why was I so uptight?

I didn't think it had anything to do with the reticent side of my personality. To me feeling reticent was not the same as feeling reluctant. When I was reluctant to show my emotions, I was deliberately holding back. When feeling reticent, I moved forward, going toward whatever called me. Often it was a need for quiet time alone, to write, to daydream, to putter, to wander in the natural world or into peaceful hours of reading.

Still, my old pattern of holding back my emotions in order to control my speech and to keep other people from going out of control wasn't working anymore. It never did work.

Ann was aware I blocked my emotions, and she tried to help me. Before Luke died, he noticed I was distancing my emotions more than usual. He questioned me, and I was beginning to open up and talk about it. I was getting better at identifying my emotions and letting my feelings run through me. But I was still stuck.

It was time for me to take my walls down, all of them.

Somehow the conversation about honesty I was having with myself led me to thinking about love. Intimate love was scary territory. It gave me the all-consuming job of dealing with all of my emotions, with another person involved who was dealing with all of their own emotions, and our emotions got tangled up together.

When I thought about the three boys, men, I'd loved deeply, I felt a pit in my stomach, so I avoided thinking about them. The first was a boy I'd loved when I was a teenager. Our relationship ended peacefully. We both felt ready to go our own ways. I wasn't holding any sorrow or regret, only sweet love for the time we were together. The second person I'd loved was Luke, complicated platonic love. And the third love was my husband, extra-strength complicated love. Three loves woven together within me.

But somewhere early in life, I had formed an idea, believing it was honorable to love only one partner at a time. The next love could begin only after I had erased my emotions. When I was young, it made sense to clear the field, get rid of any emotions I was holding onto from a previous relationship. The problem was this notion left me with a heart of barren land. Each time I began loving another person, I plowed my emotions under and cleared the space in order to begin anew.

When Marie suggested I pay attention to anything I was avoiding, I let emotions I'd felt long ago back in. After all those fallow years, the land in my heart was rich, ready to grow in abundance. I began to see how each good love builds upon the next and expands our capacity to love.

I thought about how over the years Mary Lou had figured out how to help me learn to love myself. It made a great difference; I felt safe. I was becoming a good listener, without worrying about what I was going to say next. I had begun to talk about my emotions and to write essays sharing my feelings, exploring my thoughts, without worrying about how someone might react.

When I stopped tossing away old love and took the saddle off of the emotions I was trying to tame, the landscape within me grew abundant with self-acceptance, with love, and I didn't need to name it or control it or assign meaning. It just was, and I could let it be, and this was a strong beginning for me.

40

SEARCHING FOR A
PLACE TO STAND

Unless I say something to make it clear, most people have no idea I
straddle between two races of people who historically, ethnically, and
culturally do not think the same.

Bill and Luke believed that writing from my own Native standpoint
would pave the way for me to become stronger in my personal life.
They were right. But when editors began inviting me to write opinion pieces on Thanksgiving, Halloween, and Columbus Day, from a
Native point of view and on other topics over which Native society
and white society clash, some of my white friends became offended
by what I had to say.

These were relationships I valued. But they couldn't comprehend
why Native America held views that differed greatly from those of
many within white America.

"Can't you take steps to at least dial back the level of 'Indianness'
signaled in your writing and make an effort to soften your opinions?"
one friend suggested.

"But you are both white and Indian. Can you find a middle ground?"
another friend asked.

"Sometimes I forget that you aren't one of us," my cousin said.
She was a cousin on my mother's side of the family, a white woman.
We were the same age and had grown up together. The way "one of

us" slid out sounded like she said "us and them" on a regular basis, separating white people from people of color.

Her words seared me, like stepping on a hot coal. Silence fell over the room. Everyone was staring at me. No one moved. The expression on her face gave no sign that she was worried about my reaction. Thoughts about how Indians didn't trust white people began marching through my mind.

I leaned forward, and we came face to face.

"Hey," I said, "what's that supposed to mean?"

One eyebrow arched up on her forehead and quivered there. "I didn't mean it to sound like that. I'm sorry," she said.

I thought about all of the other times when things like this came up. When Bill was alive, I went to him. We'd talked about it in one of our last conversations.

"They want me to calm down my Native thinking, and I don't want to have to pretend myself away," I said.

Bill stared at me for a moment that long-ago day.

"You're going to have to stand your ground." he said, "Native American people are one of the most underrepresented and misunderstood minorities in all of North America and are too often depicted as having existed during colonization and western expansion, as if belonging only in the past but not as people in the world today."

I sighed.

Bill inhaled, and gasping for air, he adjusted the oxygen tube in his nose.

"Playing down Blackness or being Native is a common strategy, but it takes a psychic toll," he said. "Maybe even a greater toll now, as people calibrate identity more carefully." Bill closed his eyes and shook his head.

That long-ago afternoon I came to understand that I would never be part white, the same as I would never be part Indian. I was a mixed-blood, and it carried its own racial identity. The mixed-blood attitude has a long history of not being trusted by either Indian or white. It has carried the label of double-dealing half-breeds, and mixed-bloods had to choose against one of their bloodlines.

I didn't want to have to choose for blood, yet I did. I was carrying a long legacy, and it was becoming too heavy of a load.

Something opened in me. Walking forward, I would choose for love, for compassion, and for spirit and not against one of my bloodlines.

When I found my way into the elders' writing circle Bill led on Friday mornings, I could never have guessed the friendships I made would carry me for many decades and would become the hands that shaped me into the writer I am today.

My elder friends had spent countless hours guiding me, helping me understand the ancestors were grooming me to perform work while I'm on this earth. Our ancestors are helping all of us. Everyone has the ability to be guided if we are willing to take the time to listen. It can be as simple as hearing and feeling a call to gardening or as complicated as being called into politics.

It took me quite some time to hear, and then I was able to see that writing was a path for me within the seven ways. It was the way I did my work in a world divided by two deeply different worldviews. Native America and America are often in conflict, two groups of people with differing philosophies. The space dividing them vibrates with tensions of race, historical trauma, broken treaties, politics, and different ideas about the true meaning of land.

On one side land was viewed as lifeless materials available for the taking. Water, soil, minerals, and wildlife were often ignored in the name of greed and corporate wealth.

On the other side is an ancient story of nourishing the land. Fertile soil, fresh water, and clear air a gift to all beings, and they must be respected. Native people view wildlife as our relatives. This required gratitude, reverence, and respect. Water and land are sacred. Living breathing entities we must care for. We take care of the land, and in return she cares for us. Land is our mother, our cradle, our teacher, our garden, our medicine, our church, and our grave.

Yet despite the differences, Native people have survived. In a world of questions, Native American literature offered answers and helped ensure survival. While there would always be conflict between the white mindset and Native lifeways, there were great numbers of white

Americans who could see and feel from the Native point of view. Americans, standing together, choosing heart and spirit.

For the longest time, I thought my writing was not important unless I tackled the big topics on a large canvas. Then I began receiving invitations from other authors to contribute chapters to anthologies, books with works from a collective of Native writers.

Searching for a place to stand, I discovered what I enjoyed most as a writer was being part of a collective of voices. Collaborating with other Native writers, with each of us telling our single story, working together to bring forth a whole.

41

ON THE WAY HOME

Collaborating with other Native writers unlocked many doors for me. I was at a community event when my path crossed with John Trudell, a Native American author and activist.

John was one of the speakers that day, and he said: "Whatever happens to us in our life is there to help make us stronger. It doesn't matter if it is something glorious or something traumatic, it will make us stronger. If we don't understand this, our weakness will become stronger, but if we understand, our strength will become stronger."

When I heard John say this, it was like finding a rope tied from the barn to the house in a blizzard, and it led me home to my deepest self. My path on the seven ways had led me to the tallest mountain, and I had a beautiful view of my life.

I'm a person who could see my life experiences as a series of heartaches. When you count up the hard knocks and unlucky things that have come my way, the numbers stack up.

Still, there is plenty I'm thankful for and have gained moving me forward in a good direction. I was brought into a community of strong Native people, women and men, who fed my soul, and I've come out knowing only how lucky I've been and aware that the good things in my life will always outweigh the bad.

42

THE INDIGENOUS WAY OF COMPREHENDING

I was working on a manuscript for an anthology containing a collection of works by Native writers, and my writing stalled. My work needed to show the Indigenous way of comprehending and understanding. I was feeling my way along, with a strong sense of being able to feel what I wanted to write, but I didn't know how to put it into words.

When I was having trouble writing, I headed outdoors. An offshore breeze was blowing, bringing the scent of salty sea air. I picked my way along the rocky path in my backyard, surveying the leafy garden greens and searching the tomato and zucchini plants. It was too soon for tomatoes, but the zucchini had begun to share with us. I bent low to the earth and said good morning to the yellow squash blossoms. From a branch high above, a red-shouldered hawk watched me. The mountain sage growing in my yard was fragrant with its cleansing and healing. The scent touched me deep behind my belly, and I thought about how Auntie always told us to put a thing in our holy middle to feel it. I plucked a few sage leaves and said thank-you to the sage by plucking a hair from my head and letting it fall to the ground near her roots.

In the Native ways of living and being, according to how I was taught, we humans are the younger brothers and sisters of creation, and the plant world, minerals, and members of the animal kingdom are our relatives. They are our relatives because we are all alive on the same Earth Mother and get water, air, food, and shelter from her. From Auntie's stories, I knew we saw the universe as having both a visible and invisible world, and spirit worked with Creator to help us.

I harvested arugula, cilantro, zucchini, and red serrano peppers. While the land we lived on could not sustain us completely, she fed us well.

Next, I foraged my freezer and retrieved a loaf of sourdough bread. It was our last loaf, but if we went easy, it would provide us with lunch sandwiches for the next couple of days.

After lunch I dug into my secret stash. On the last day of my life, I want to have had a piece of dark chocolate; therefore, whenever possible, I ate a piece.

After lunch I returned to my writing desk and spent the afternoon writing paragraphs and deleting them. Every afternoon I worked on the manuscript, stopping just before sunset, then I headed outside. The sky had turned from rosy to lavender and was opening into dark blue. The wind came up, and I got to thinking about how when Ann talked about the traditional knowledge of plants used for making baskets, she spoke about where each reed grew. Since making baskets was of great importance to California Indian communities, she knew that certain reeds often grew on several sites. If the women in the village could not make, or mend, baskets wherever their camps were, the food supply could be at risk, possibly meaning starvation.

Ann knew when was the best time to harvest and what other plants lived near the different reeds and about all of their relationships with other plants. She talked about the birds that were indigenous to the area and how they built their nests with the fibers often used in basketmaking. She shared stories about the origin myths of the reeds used for making baskets and about the teaching stories of how they got their names. She could understand and teach not only with her mind, but she could also feel the knowledge within her body, and the understanding was woven into her instincts, her passion, her spirit.

Within the Indigenous way of thinking, we live every day in a sacred manner without separation between spirituality and daily living. Spirituality is so much a part of Native lives, it cannot be distinguished from our lives.

It came to me then. The Indigenous way Ann was able to comprehend and understand was strongest in me. But it wasn't fully developed.

43

ON THE MEDICINE TRAIL

I was doing a great deal of writing and thinking, with too many thoughts churning inside my mind. I couldn't always get away by myself for a few days to be alone and silent to clear my mind. I'd begun to realize silence needed to come from within.

Marie had stopped reminding me, but the look in her eyes held a warning, calling me to remember that a spiritual life manifests in the day-to-day world and that if I kept my mind too wrapped up, I wouldn't develop the spiritual awareness I needed.

The morning I stopped by to talk with Ann, the air was fog soft-ened, blurring the boundaries between the earth and the sky. Her home was open to her many friends, and there was always someone arriving or leaving. When I showed up on her front doorstep, she smiled down at me.

"Oh, it's you," she said. She tilted her head to one side. "What's wrong?" She took off her glasses, motioned for me to come in, and pointed at the hard-backed chair between her weaving loom and the dining room table. "Sit."

I sat on the edge of the chair and told her about my wild mind.

She said, "When you wake up in the morning, before you read the paper or turn on the news, before you check your email or listen to phone messages, first, go outside. Look at the sky, feel the air, listen for bird sounds."

The next morning, instead of thinking of all of the things I had to do the minute my eyes opened, I began my day by praying to the earth and relaxing for a few minutes.

Most of the time I woke up early, before sunrise. My usual morning routine was to work for a couple of hours and then go for a walk. I decided to walk first, to let my mind clear out and settle down. The first morning I began my new ritual, the moon was still out, in a waning crescent phase, solitary in the sky, with only a small edge of her illuminated, replete with power. She stared at me, and I stared back.

By the time I was dressed and ready to go, the sun was beginning to rise. My dog grew tense with happiness when I laced up my tennis shoes. Often I walked a two-mile loop in my neighborhood. Other days I walked along the shoreline at the beach, soothed by the rhythm of the waves, ocean spray, and mist falling around me. My mind emptied, and the tide carried my thoughts out to sea.

Sometimes I walked a path near the Old Mission. The early-morning silence was so intense, I stopped to listen. I paused for a few minutes near Mission Creek, in a place lightly touched, almost rural, near the sedimentary sandstone walls brought by Father Junípero Serra's Franciscans. The beige-pink stone spoke, telling sad stories. It took me a few minutes to get myself quiet enough to hear what it had to say, while lizards scurried past my feet.

But on the days when I couldn't walk anywhere at all or set aside a sizable amount of time to be alone, to be silent and wait for my thoughts to clear, and when I only had a few minutes to spare, I stepped outside, or I headed to the nearest window. I'd look up at the sky, and instead of trying to block out any noise, like I had in the past, now I softened my gaze and took in everything around me. I listened to the sounds—the neighbor's dog barking, the hum of the freeway in the distance, an occasional train passing through—and I let the sounds become a tapestry of background noise.

When I let go of the idea of trying to hush the outside world, it was possible to grow calm and relaxed because I felt the silence within.

At those times when I had a million things to do and was feeling so scattered that I couldn't enjoy each moment before it was spent, I gave myself the gift of twenty minutes, and I went outside and sat down with my feet on the earth and focused on how my feet felt against the grass or the dirt. I looked around.

What did I see? What did I smell? What colors were around me? Red and yellow leaves sharing afternoon light. Twigs breaking under my feet. A purple flower I cannot name, so delicate. The scent of freshly mowed grass. The sun calling my name. Dusk falling fast.

When I was simply aware of what was happening around me, somehow it began to train me to be fully present in the moment.

After releasing the cluttered thoughts in my mind and letting go of any worries I was holding onto, even if only for a few minutes, I felt relaxed and calm. In time I discovered this form of meditation rejuvenated me almost as much as if I'd taken a short nap. It was a practice I could take with me anywhere, and it only required a few minutes to feel recharged.

44

TANGLED THOUGHTS

It was fall, and I was rooted in my new pattern of walking at sunrise, when the air was cool and blue-bellied clouds hung low over the mountains. I was growing more skilled with clearing my mind, yet there were still days when my thoughts were heavy saddlebags.

I walked faster than usual on this morning, with my dog at my side, thinking about a workshop I had attended the day before. It was a session on navigating discussions on race and ethnicity. Within the first hour, we were given an icebreaker assignment. We were given a topic, asked to partner with someone, to take turns and give each person five minutes to speak.

The white woman I partnered with went first. When it was my turn, she would not let me say more than a few words before she began asking me a series of rapid-fire, deeply personal questions. Each time I answered, she fired yet another question at me. When I told her that I grew up in Southeast Los Angeles and my family was American Indian, she interrupted and said: "But you don't look like you are Native American. And you didn't grow up on a reservation. How much Indian are you?"

She was asking me to tell her my blood quantum. It's an inappropriate question. Indian blood quantum laws in the United States and the former thirteen colonies were used as a tactic to reduce the number of Indians and Native nations and resulted in forced assimilation.

The woman kept talking, but I stopped listening. By now I could feel my hackles going up. This scene and similar scenes play out thousands of times, over and again for me and for my Native family members and friends, by white peers who think that in order to be a "real Indian," we need to live on our reservation.

My mind began to unsheathe my tomahawk. I wanted to chop her words to bits. Instead, I did what I always do when someone becomes very aggressive and challenges whether or not I am Indian enough. I shut down. I could feel myself shrinking, getting smaller and smaller, fading away.

But her next statement startled me alert.

"What you mean is that you have Native American ancestry—now I understand."

But she didn't understand anything at all. Suddenly, I had a lightning bolt moment, and my life unfolded before me as if I were watching a film.

First marker moment. It's 1956, and I am three years old. I'm in the back seat. My dad is driving, and my mother is beside him, but then she's screaming. Some white guys are pulling my dad out of the car, beating him. Mexican guys come to help my dad. We are safe now. I will replay this memory over and again. A decade later I will understand. Because he was a brown boy, an Indian boy, with a white girl. I was in grade school, attending the Compton City School District when I figured this out.

By age ten the pattern is set. I have learned that everyone who isn't white feels safe to me. White feels like walking a razor's edge. You had to watch yourself at all times. Be aware. Watch for clues. Make up stories to protect your mixed-blood, undereducated family. If you don't pass the tests issued by the mothers and fathers, they won't allow you to play with their white daughters. Me, a rough-around-the-edges girl with skin so light, assumed to be white as long as she answers the questions right. But the mixed-race families and the brown-skinned families would always take you in, without asking too many questions.

Second marker moment. It's 1963, and a new family moves into the house across the street, German immigrants, with a kind boy, my age. Neighborhood gossip issued from the first tier says they had belonged to Hitler's Youth, long ago, and had moved to America to escape all of that. The taunting begins. Nazi signs are painted all over the house. Broken, the family moves away.

I think about my German ethnicity, about my German great-grandfather and my German-Jewish great-grandmother, immigrating to the United States before the war, and I can feel the hate they endured.

Third marker moment. It's 1965, and the sun is an orange haze, and the sky turned black. The Watts riots have begun. I'm twelve years old. The city of Watts borders Compton; it's nearby, not far away. Smoke is thick in the air, and I worry about friends and everyone else in danger. Later that year I will learn that although women were guaranteed the right to vote in 1920 by the Nineteenth Amendment, in some southern states African American women were unable to freely exercise their right to vote until 1965.

The final straw. It's 1972, and I'm nineteen, unmarried, and pregnant. In a social welfare office, I list my race as American Indian. The father of the baby is also American Indian, but I will not reveal his name. Instead, I write down that the father is unknown.

The welfare officer, a white woman, gave me a lecture, telling me I'm trash for sleeping with any Tom, Dick, or Harry. I huddled in the hallway and cried. Another social worker, a Black woman, came to check on me, and when I told her what happened, she hugged me and said that I was not the first pregnant girl and Lord knows I won't be the last and not to pay any mind to anyone who treats me like I'm less than.

That year, 1972, was also the year that American Indian Movement (AIM) organizers and local Native parents, motivated by prejudice in the child welfare system and hostility in the public schools, started their own community school. The story of these survival schools, unfolding through the voices of activists, teachers, and families, is also a history of AIM's founding and of its long-term effect on Indian people's lives.

Maybe the social worker who said I was trash was just a spiteful woman and it had nothing to do with racism. Yeah. Maybe.

Meanwhile, while I was in the middle of making the connection that white privilege is the ability to attribute hateful behavior to isolated incidents, classism, bad luck, or just a bad social worker with a bad attitude, the white woman sitting next to me in the workshop was silent now. She stared at me, blinking, waiting for me to speak. Our conversation about my race and ethnicity seemed to have been left on a street corner on the other side of the Continental Divide.

She glanced over at me. When I caught her eye, she looked away.

I leaned closer to her, smiled, and felt a deep place inside me begin to rise.

I could choose for love, for compassion, and for spirit.

I put my hand on her arm.

"You were asking me about growing up?"

"Yeah," she said.

I laughed and leaned back in my seat.

"Talk to my grandma, and you will hear stories about me in diapers taking my first steps in mixed-race, mixed-blood America." I unclenched my hands and wrapped them around the edge of my closed notebook and took a deep breath. "I'm Cherokee, Lenape, Seneca, a 100 percent mixed-blood American Indian, with German and Jewish ancestry, and I grew up in Los Angeles, with roots in Oklahoma."

I was able to pull myself into the moment, into what was happening all around us. This was my opportunity to learn a better way to deal with aggressive behavior hurled at me, and I didn't want to waste it. It was painful, but I stayed open.

By the time I had walked the first mile, my morning thoughts were untangled. I looked up at the sky; the sun was covered with high gray clouds. I shrugged my shoulders and tightened my cinch on yesterday. The air was filled with birdsong, and my dog was panting happily. Then I made the decision to set my weary thoughts free. In the second mile of my walk, only the colors emerging in the scrub oak and the smell of mountain sage called me. Called me home.

45

WINTER COUNT

Mary Lou, Irene, and Marie lived long lives. First, Mary Lou walked on, and I turned to the sea, sky, and to the wind as poetry and as ceremony while grieving her death. She had walked the sacred hoop, and her community had extended to the stars.

Then Irene crossed over to the other side. Within her lifetime she continued to hold grudges and allowed anger to rule her. She had grown older and had become elderly. She never did gain the interest to do the spiritual work needed in order to grow right as an elder.

Marie's spiritual life continued to grow deep roots, and she became proficient in the way of the ritual. She never talked about it. Her actions served as a model for younger women on the path. Before she died, I knew she had entered her period of mastery.

She would not want me to share details about her tribal identity. She was private in that she would not want to be known as a leader or as an authority figure, just to be known as grandmother, stepping in to pick up and help another woman on the path in need.

Though if she knew I was writing about the part of our story that is mine to share, I believe she would have said, "Hooray." She said hooray often when she was happy with a story I was writing. If you had asked her about the seven ways and beliefs she lived by, she would have told you that each woman has specific nuanced ways of living and believing that are shaped by their tribe's, or culture's, worldviews or by the religion, race, and ethnicity they are descended from, and these play out in the way they interact, portray themself, and they are how we retain our identity.

Marie would not want others to see her grandmother's seven ways as "the only way." She would only want women to know there are many paths that can be followed to grow strong with the seven values she aspired to.

Turning to nature—spending time with the moon; gazing at the night sky, cold, clear, and studded with stars; or gardening in the rain, with my dog at my side rooting in the mud—became my ritual each time someone I loved walked on.

Bill, my cousin Victor, Luke, my son Jay, along with my circle of elder women friends, with one after the other dying, gave me much opportunity to create my grieving and healing rituals.

Ann was well into her eighties and was rapidly growing frail but with a hardy mind and rock-solid determination. I was in my late sixties, with plenty of vigor and strong enough to do almost anything I wanted. Compared to Ann, I was practically still just a kid. Yet I had begun the passage; my journey into older age was underway.

Each morning I walked my usual two-mile loop, but my body no longer moved as easily as it had in the past. My face had grown fragile and my skin more wrinkled. It was a time of assessing aims. Coming to an understanding, an acceptance of what I had and had not achieved. A time of peace, of power, a time of forgiveness and compassion, of giving up old patterns, surrendering to changes, embracing changes in preparation for the major changes that will come. Learning the lessons of the giveaway.

Viewing this period of time in my life as my "winter count" reminded me of the Lakota tradition that many Native communities had taken up as a term and a practice—noting the list of those who die in a year.

With so many of my close friends walking on, I became more aware my reserves were no longer limitless and that where I put my time mattered. Choices. Decisions. What book writing projects did I want to put forth? And to be living after I was not living?

Each year I gave myself a word theme and let it take me to experiences that were unexpected. Some years I was specifically focused.

But this time my goal was to let myself dream more, to lean into the moment and be open to what comes. I wanted to let go of any particular end goal and be willing to flow with the unexpected ripples and outcomes that arrived and to step out of my comfort zone and be open to possibilities.

Before I had a chance to select my word, my life began to erupt with many changes, and I had no interest in answering from a place of fear or control. The word *change* had selected me, and I leaned into the changes taking place. Some of the most important things I had planned for were not unfolding as I had expected or wanted.

Our income decreased. Hard-earned money we had saved was spent on necessary life expenses. I had been living frugally for the past few years, saving instead of spending, and it made me grumpy to meet expenses with money slated for future hopes and dreams.

Cancer and other health issues surfaced for my husband.

The dog got sick. Vet bills.

Still, the good things outnumbered the bad. My husband's health stabilized. The dog's health improved. I had my lucky money saved so we could pay the bills. I continued to break old bad habits and developed new behaviors that better served me.

Sometimes there were long stretches when it was difficult for me to know if I was still on the path following the seven ways. Then I understood I was trying too hard. I was looking for markers, a road map, something to show my progress, my gain. These thoughts proved I'd taken a detour because I was thinking with my physical, rational mind. Trying to be in control. Instead of allowing the spiritual end to guide me.

As long as I stayed faithful to upholding the seven values, there was every reason to believe I was inching my way along on the path of the seven ways. What I had gained in the years when my son lived with a brain tumor and in the years after his death was the confidence to know I would always be able to deal with whatever came, that strength comes from unimaginable sources, and that it was much easier for me to give than to receive.

I followed Ann's suggestion and completed a sermon-writing workshop and spent six months within a liberal progressive worship ministry team, where I was free to express my Indigenous views. Next, I attended a yearlong curriculum centering on navigating compassionate conversations about race and ethnicity with mixed groups of white people and people of color. After the course ended, I accepted the volunteer role as facilitator for the next session. I was moving out of my comfort zone often enough to make the uncomfortable begin to feel comfortable.

I came to a deeper understanding of how volunteerism was the backbone of community and the rent we pay for the space we take up on this good earth. After three decades volunteering within my communities, I began to understand I was no longer a distance runner. Now my strength was sprinting. Giving my all to complete a section of the volunteer work needing to be done and then passing the baton and giving myself a pause, a hiatus before accepting the next volunteer assignment.

When one volunteer assignment ended, I waited a couple of weeks before saying yes to another volunteer job. Without these quiet times, I might not have noticed the orb weaver garden spider who spun her web near my back door. Because she was never around during the day, I became a night watcher. I checked on her before I went to bed and again early in the morning, when it was still dark.

Once I found her in the center of her web at twilight. But usually, she arrived after dusk and left before sunrise. For days I was heart deep in the role of observer, grounded in a regular practice of watching. Since I saw the spider only briefly in the dark of night, never staying long so that I would not disturb her, what I was really observing was the state of her web. It was perfectly formed at dawn and always in disarray, tattered and torn, as the day wore on. Each night she repaired her web, and it was spectacular.

Two weeks later, when I felt renewed, I was invited to teach a six-week creative writing class for elementary school children. I said yes and agreed to volunteer my time.

For most American Indian people, a core belief is that we must care for ourselves first, before we can give to others. Otherwise, we will be depleted, and we won't have anything of value to offer.

After a lifetime of giving, I was finally beginning to figure out how to become open and receive. The lessons came in bits and pieces from numerous friends. From the story I heard about a rabbi who said that all of the experiences, teachings, and gifts offered to us in our earlier years, the ones we were not yet ready to receive then, were sitting near our heart, waiting for our heart to break and let them in.

I needed to allow vulnerability and heartbreak to pierce me in order to let the light in, to let the dark in, and within the mix came joy.

I learned from the words of a Mexican actor and activist in Mexico who said that in order for her to manage all the poverty and injustice she sees, she must meditate; otherwise, she would not be able to stay sane and cope with it. She said in meditation she gives thanks for her pain and sensitivity and for realizing what goes on. And that if she didn't feel the pain, it would mean she didn't care and was beginning to harden. Her words guided me. I'd much rather feel pain, sorrow, and worry than be indifferent.

I couldn't always volunteer to do as much as I'd like or to bring forth needed change in the world, but I was aware, deeply aware, and I cared. I began giving myself a few quiet minutes each day to give thanks for my awareness.

There was a time when I didn't know how to feed my spirit and ended up muffling it with demands and distractions and staying busy, instead of stilling the center.

I tossed out my to-do list, canceled unnecessary appointments, and gave myself more quiet hours each week to be silent and listen within.

At the end of each workday, instead of trying to get more and more done, I sat outside in the twilight watching the sky and the light change from day to night. The wind came up, and the chilly air embraced me. In the light of the stars and the moon penetrating the night, I began addressing my fears, and one after the other I tackled them.

Each phase of the moon, the crescent of the first quarter to the almost full three-quarter moon, called me, and I saw how each phase lights up the earth in a different way, her effect on the waters, and my emotions, and the way she lights up the shadow side of life.

In Native cultures the moons do not follow today's twelve-month calendar. Instead, there are thirteen moons, and they follow the seasons. September brought a full moon two days after the equinox, relating to change, the influence of the thirteenth moon and the way she heralds change, bringing times of transition and new opportunity.

I would continue on my quest to gain deeper knowledge of the traditional stories, the medicine stories, Auntie told me when I was growing up. But I would not write or share my discoveries. What knowledge I gained would not be mine to give away.

In the daylight dragonflies came and hovered over the pond.

I was invited to deliver the sermon–inspirational talk I wrote using storytelling to share the pathways I had cultivated to bring pockets of calm, tranquility, and spiritual renewal in a chaotic world.

The memory I wanted to last and be passed on is that I was a person who was not always a busy, frantic woman with worry wrinkles around her eyes. I also wanted it to go down in history that I was relaxed and fun to be with.

With so many of those I was close to having completed their lives on earth, my circle of women friends had grown smaller. I heard Auntie's voice in my mind, reminding me. "The moment we let the spiritual world know we are in need, opportunity and teachers will arrive."

To begin making new friends, I made it a priority to put myself in a wider range of situations and places where I would have an opportunity to meet a variety of women.

At first I went in search of women my age, someone who might mirror my own image back to me, to find someone similar to me. And then I remembered how long ago I'd stepped away from my comfort zone and allowed myself to be drawn to women whom I perceived to be different, women who might have intimidated me in a previous time of my life. It brought me into a community of elder women who fed my soul.

They embraced me and guided me through the cycles of my life, from motherhood toward elderhood. Over three decades these women lifted me from grief, instructed me in living, taught me how to find richness in living every stage of my life, and showed me how to age from youth into beauty. I felt beautiful. The women I had grown to love all had grandmother faces and flying clouds of white hair. They grew smaller as they aged, wrinkling into buttery skin. But I only saw how beautiful they were and how they were at home in their bodies in a way I was becoming more familiar with.

To find new friendships, I began looking for ways to connect with others and let go of my old habit of viewing differences as an obstacle. Slowly, my circle of friends expanded and included women who were younger than me and a few who were older, all with qualities I admired and hoped to gain.

Now I was a grandmother. As if by magic, assorted little people were tromping through my house again, requiring snacks, Band-Aids, water. Pulling books off the shelves and asking me to read one more story, and then we snuggled with books on our laps.

I had a knowing feeling that I was beginning to come full circle, with an understanding of how endings lead to beginnings, and I could feel myself within Indigenous time and understood how forward time is an illusion. I was every age I ever have been. I was eleven riding the waves on my raft in the ocean. I was fourteen and seventeen on my friend's surfboard, slicing through the surf. Thirty-five, swimming with my kids at the river, with our Newfoundland dog. We are holding onto her collar as she tows us to shore. And I'm sixty-eight, sixty-nine, swimming in the waves with my grandchildren. What a wonderful life, I thought.

46

FORTY-FIVE WINTERS

The secret to a long marriage is to never get divorced. Marriage is complicated. Neither Gary nor I am the type who could come together and become as one. We both had strong personalities and many conflicts, yet we gave favors and bought each other time.

We were handed a difficult parenthood, and we loved each other enough not to abandon the other. There were difficult years, but always there was love and caring. We allowed each other to grow and change, and together we learned to provide the space to become what we must.

It was a marriage lasting forty-five years at this writing. Yet we always said we had three marriages. The one we had for the first fifteen years, the marriage that took place in the middle years, and the marriage we had now.

Why do some people view a relationship or a marriage that does not remain in its exact original pattern as tragic? When we were in our late sixties, we began to find ourselves more alike, two people listening to each other.

As often happens when people come very close to dying yet are able to walk away physically unharmed, everything petty bothering us before stopped mattering.

Our turning point came the day we were on the road, a few miles from home, when a driver on the wrong side of a two-lane highway raced toward us. Gary was driving, but I saw the car first and tried to warn Gary. But I could not speak, and the sound coming out of me made a deep guttural noise.

My throaty growl caught Gary's attention. Without a moment to consider, he made a sharp right turn. Our tires did not screech, and the car didn't roll. We lurched out of the way, as the wrong-way driver sped by, inches from our car. I could feel the velocity and the rush of wind, and then something, Creator, Spirit, carried us out of danger. We sat on the side of the road, stunned. Silent at first and, after a long pause, talking in low voices. Looking at the landscape around us, at the narrow shoulder on this stretch of the highway, a safety net to catch us. Whereas in other places on this road there wasn't a shoulder. Aware we were now forever changed, on a different trajectory. We sat on the side of the road for a long time before continuing on our way.

Gary said, "Anything and everything that happens in our lives after this is a bonus."

Thereafter, we viewed every single thing we experienced in life as extra. Extra opportunities we were lucky to have because we were still alive.

For me, since I saw the car coming first, I believe I had what is called a life review. When we came around the curve, I saw a black car ahead of us in the distance, but it was coming toward us, fast. I'm positive it was only a few seconds between the time I saw headlights, not taillights, made the loud guttural growl alerting Gary, and he steered the car out of the way. Yet in those seconds I lived a lifetime. I remember my detailed thoughts in those seconds, the memories playing and the calm I felt surrounding me. Thinking this must be a life exit, happening right now, and curious thoughts about how I never guessed this was how I would die. Also thinking it would be all right, yet if there was a pathway back to living, I would take it. Just then our car veered out of the way, and we were safe.

In the weeks after coming close to dying, we began having many lively conversations, making peace with the past. On this day Gary was talking about not feeling heard.

"As a kid, I never felt heard," he said. "Once, when I was upset about something serious, I called my mom at work. She told me we would talk later. Meanwhile, I should call Dial-a-Prayer, and she gave me the number."

Gary had told me this story a few times before in our years together. Yet since we were having a conversation about feeling heard, I wanted to make sure he knew I was listening. It was heartbreaking, and I said what I could to soothe old wounds still waiting to heal.

"The next time we are having a discussion and if you don't feel heard, is there something I can say or do to let you know I'm listening?" I asked.

"It's hard to say," he answered. "I'll think about it and let you know." His brow furrowed. "Did you feel like your parents listened to you?" he asked.

"No, I got slapped when I tried to express myself. They didn't want to hear what I had to say."

Laughing, Gary said: "They heard you all right. But they didn't want to hear what you had to say. But you found a way around the roadblock."

"What's that?" I asked. I set down my glasses and looked at Gary.

"Well, you found a way to be heard—you became a writer."

His comment struck us both as screamingly funny. We began laughing, and for years after, when I thought about his comment, my laughter began again.

47

DANCING TO REMEMBER

It was powwow weekend. The wind was spilling through the tree leaves. In my mind I could see Irene getting ready to dance. Now she was dancing in the spirit world. Later in the afternoon, Ann would join me. Meanwhile, I was alone, thinking back on the years. Time merged with timelessness. Memories circled and carried me to a day four decades ago, when I stood on this good land, near the oak tree for the first time, with my young children gathered about.

The same tree I stood under today. I leaned my back against this oak. This tree, giver of life. She raised a Native community with song, dance, and prayer. We returned to this land, to this tree, in October every year. Laughter, flirting, and romance in lives young and old took place all around her. She stands sentry. Her autumn-softened leaves, swept up from a cool mountain breeze, fell gently on American Indian fathers holding sleeping babies. Mothers trading stories, their shiny cut beads reflecting light while braiding their children's hair, with feathers in the colors of the earth, trailing.

There were difficult times, too, for this oak tree, when she witnessed wildfires raging, drought years with dust rising against the clear sky. The times when her branches sheltered human arguments and angry outbursts, but mostly, she was surrounded by love and caring.

I stood high upon a flat rock, remembering. Filling my lungs with sweet fragrances of the damp Mother Earth. Feeling my body grow light, like the feathers of the red-tailed hawk touching the soft clouds.

For four decades I had walked gently, a guest on this good land making up the traditional Chumash homeland. I remembered Auntie's words about how each person is a link to history and that when it comes to powwows, all Native people gathered around the arena are participating as we form a circle around the drums, singers, and dancers. And how every American Indian person at the powwow is connected, making a statement that American Indian people are still here. This was our celebration of life past, present, and future.

48

TOMOL EVENING

When we returned from Limuw—Santa Cruz Island—at first I only wanted natural light. It was past ten when I rinsed the salt water from my hair. Moonlight fell from the open window, a flood of light from above. I was still under the influence of sea tides springing strong.

I came to spend four days and four nights on the island, to let come what may. I wanted to be helpful to Ann. She was teaching Native children and adults basket weaving, beadwork, and storytelling. She was still hearty but needed help fetching things and getting from here to there. I was learning as she taught me how to be helpful and to grow old in a beautiful way.

Used to be, when you walked on the island of Santa Cruz and looked around, all the land you could see was Chumash Indian land. The island was once home to the largest population of island Chumash, with a highly developed complex society and lifeways, with marine harvest and trade with the mainland. Island Chumash produced shell beads used for currency. Grasses and roots for making baskets and other necessities for living were there for the taking.

And so, apparently, was the land. Historical records show that by 1853 a large herd of sheep was brought to the island.

The Civil War significantly increased the demand for wool, and by 1864 some twenty-four thousand sheep overgrazed the hills and valleys of Santa Cruz Island. Some of the early buildings from sheep ranching still stand.

For the next four days, the island would again be filled with Indians. We had come to honor the Chumash peoples' annual channel crossing from the mainland to the Channel Islands.

A camp village was put up, where basketmaking, cordage making, song, prayer, and storytelling would take place. The first day about fifty Indians gathered. By Saturday, the day the tomol arrived, there would be nearly two hundred of us, and the adage "A single bracelet does not jangle alone" described us. The connectedness we had to each other was so much a part of our lives, it couldn't be distinguished from our lives.

Although I am not Chumash, for forty-three years I lived near the ocean in an area that made up the traditional Chumash homeland. I hold the culture, traditions, and history of the Chumash people in my heart. For my Chumash friends, this was their heritage, their landscape of time.

There is power on the island. When we left the campsite village and walked to the rim of the island, first there was silence. Ravens and seagulls at the water's edge dipped and wheeled and dived. We went for sunset swims under a sky turned pink. With much island and ocean and so few people, there was a lazy wag of space. I floated in the sea with my head surrounded by gulls and fledglings.

The next morning at dawn, we woke to sunrise singers. A high sweet trill of voices, abalone beads swaying, carrying songs from the ancestors. The singers were letting us know it was time to gather for the sunrise ceremony.

Later in the day, as we waited for the paddlers to arrive, I stood with others on the shore and felt the sun rise from my heart. I'd known two of the paddlers, a male and a female crew member, since they were babies, and I'd watched them grow to be strong, beautiful, kind, and responsible adults. Now I was a grandmother, moving toward elderhood, and I knew the world that I would one day leave behind was in good hands.

For a moment I was returned to 1994, when these two young paddlers were small kids and our community began the American Indian Education Academy Project series "Tomol Trek," with a goal of building a modern-day recreation of a tomol. Our tomol was built by the children under the guidance of a master, in his backyard tomol-building workshop. There was a perfect balance between master and apprentice as the children sanded pieces of the vessel throughout construction.

A dozen hands moved slowly across the handle, moving toward the paddle end of an oar. Small hands, young hands, skin so smooth and maroon, peach-colored hands, muted brown, every child with a tribal memory circling her or his heart.

Back in those days, my son and daughter were two of the kids helping out. They knew about the pleasure found in working hard and seeing the good results of that work. As they sanded the pieces of wood, I watched my kids find their relationship with the tomol they had helped build. Our kids did not have to exchange their Native values for education; the tomol carried ancient memory and cultural knowledge into their present lives.

Now two of the children who attended the academy were grown-ups, and they were making the crossing in the tomol. The paddlers left the mainland at 3:00 a.m. There would be a careful change of crew three times. The moment the paddlers in the tomol came into view, my heart broke open, and I was ageless and timeless and felt the welcome arms of the ancestors.

The tomol was brought forth from the sea, and there was song and prayer.

Back at camp we prepared dinner, while island fox kept a steady eye on us. The day faded into liquid dusk, and a near harvest moon rose. We ate, talked, joked, laughed, and told stories of past crossings to the island and of "the old ways," moving through our evening together like dancers, stirring to the same rhythm. All of the people who helped make the crossing and camp village possible—those who brought and cooked the food, the fire keepers, the elders who led prayer circles and ceremonies, the singers, the dancers, and the paddlers—were honored.

Time was a continuous loop until our stay on the island came to a full-circle closure. Thankful for what I had been given yet reluctant to let go, I prepared to leave and made the rounds to say thank you to everybody who had welcomed me.

On the boat ride to the mainland, we were soaking wet, laughing. A humpback whale was sighted in the ocean. In the Chumash language my friends sang to the whale, and she surfaced.

At home in earthen shadows, rinsing off the salt water and sand, I felt the light from the moon, full and wan. I braided a pungent memory and filled my lungs and my heart with it, knowing it would permeate my body and cling to my soul as a reminder of what I felt when we were all together on the island.

49

RETURNING THE GIFT
TO THE SEA

On my morning walks along the beach, I collected seashells and carried my treasures home in my pocket and placed them in a basket.

When the basket was full, I began filling another.

Forty-three years of collecting shells from the same stretch of beach, on land that was once inhabited only by Chumash people.

When I returned home from Limuw, the inner spiritual harmony I felt made me realize having the shells was wrong.

I carried my baskets of seashells back to the beach where I had found them and placed them on the sand near the shoreline. As the tide moved in, I watched the waves wash over the shells and carry them out to sea.

50

GRATITUDE

After my memoir *Pushing Up the Sky* went out of print in 2019, at first I felt only great relief. The book was published in 2006, it had a long run, and the journey had gifted me with many opportunities.

Frequently, when I was invited to give talks within transracial adoption communities throughout the United States, I accepted generous offers to stay with families in their homes, instead of a hotel. It not only reduced the cost of accommodation expenses for the group inviting me; it provided me with glimpses into people and terrains unfamiliar to me. It gave me the opportunity to understand and see through the eyes of those who led lives different from mine.

With each city and state and among the families I stayed with, I found a multiplicity of lifestyles. These good people blended me into their lives and into their communities. From the moment I arrived at the airport until after I gave my presentation or talk, the weekend was filled with intimate conversations around kitchen tables, picnics, or buffet dinners, sharing the local foods their particular region is known for. Sightseeing, along with them telling me their stories and the local lore.

I felt as if I had stepped into a favorite book and played a role in the story line, and like the characters in a favorite book, I was always changed by the end of the visit. Humbled by the generosity these families and other individuals gave so freely. I gained greater compassion and respect for differences, and I had fun learning and exploring. For this I am deeply and tenderly thankful.

With all of these terrific experiences behind me, still, when the book sold out and I learned there would not be a second printing, instead of disappointment, I felt relief.

My private life had been returned to me. I would no longer be obligated to appear in public with the requirement of talking about controversial adoption topics or be expected to answer personal questions about my children. My children owned the rights to their adoption stories and personal histories, yet frequently, I was asked to share intimately. When I refused, it created an uncomfortable rift that I had not yet figured out how to soften. How to redirect the conversation and keep the vibe within the room upbeat, warm, and friendly. I also paid too much attention to negative reader comments and to those who tried to strike me down on the Internet.

Mulling over my thoughts, letting the years unfold, I had one of those aha moments, when I understood this was a pattern I'd fallen into fifteen years earlier, a mode of thinking I gave into and allowed it to carry me away. But I no longer felt this way.

I'm not sure when or how, but my old insecurities had vanished. Now, more often, waves of calm washed over me when I was faced with conflict and criticism.

Why had I paid so much attention to those who lead with hate? Just because someone posted something negative on the Internet did not mean it was true. It was only that person's opinion. Oftentimes the negative comment, I'd discovered, had more to say about the person who wrote it. It described their character, not mine.

While I still spent too much time living in my mind, it had become a quiet neighborhood, where I gave my thoughts more attention to kindness and gratitude. Now, when I met with adversity or criticism or when I came across a negative comment about me, it didn't toss me away. I was able to stabilize myself.

I thought back on how I had begun to grow more stable during some of the hardest years of my life. After my friend Luke died, I needed to figure out who I was without Luke, and I needed to find a new way to get there. When I found my way, something inside me began to open wide.

Then my son my died. It was an unraveling. Who was I without Jay? I needed to figure out who I was without being Jay's mother, and I needed to find a new way to get there.

With the unwavering support from everyone in my life who loves me, I have emerged stronger than I ever thought possible. Gaining full confidence that I will be able to get through anything that comes my way.

Now I feel gratitude for those who challenge me as I journey through life, and I feel gratitude for those who support me. I have come to view differing opinions and conflict as an opportunity to stretch and reach deeper and see from the other person's point of view. I might not agree with them and move over to their way of thinking, but I can walk gently, listen to what they have to say, without feeling a need to defend myself.

51

NOVEMBER

November 2019. I was well into grandmotherhood and doing my best to learn what I needed in order to grow right as an elder and to do my part to make better for the next seven generations.

While I was teaching a creative writing class for the elementary school children, I discovered the teachers, the children, and their parents had a desire to learn more about American Indian people.

Since November is National Native American Heritage month, too often teaching the rich histories of Native Peoples was braided together with Thanksgiving, which does not offer an accurate history of Native America. This limited view also did not humanize the otherwise "vanishing race" and share the stories our people would like told.

When the children's parents asked me many questions about how Native people view the story about the first Thanksgiving, I told them about the Wampanoag people. About this tribe of southern Massachusetts and how their ancestors ensured the survival of the pilgrims in New England and how they lived to regret it, but now the tribe has grown strong again.

I explained that many Native American people do not celebrate Thanksgiving. For Native People thanksgiving comes not once a year but always, for all the gifts of life. Thanksgiving Day, as it has come to be observed in the United States, is a time of mourning for many Native People. It serves as a reminder of how a gift of generosity was rewarded by theft of land and seed corn, extermination of many Native people from disease, and near total elimination of many more from forced assimilation and as a reminder of five hundred years of betrayal.

I told them Native people have a history largely untold and that gathering to give thanks for the harvest did not originate with the pilgrims; it was always our way.

In the days following, I read books to the children written by Native American authors who are working to make sure that Native lives and histories are portrayed with honesty and integrity. The stories we read showed the importance of dismissing the stereotypes of the stoic warrior, the Indian princess, the uncivilized Indian. To provide stepping-stones for the children so they could begin to see that Native American people have respect for their traditional ways and that they are also real people who work as doctors and teachers. To show the children that Native American mothers and fathers are also regular moms and dads who cook dinner, help their children with their home-work, play baseball, and are not relics of the past.

Later, while talking with the teachers and the children's parents, I reminded them that while the histories of Native People are painful to hear, the stories still need to be told and retold and never forgot-ten by generations of Americans, with the hope that through truthful knowledge of the past, we will not allow another group of people in America to have their lifeways taken from them, to have their eth-nicities and cultures erased, to be exterminated and reach near total elimination, ever again.

52

THE HARVEST DINNER

November 2019. I was gathered with my Native community for our annual November Harvest Dinner. Forty-five years ago, our Native community began this tradition. It's an intertribal gathering with traditional foods, song, dance, prayer, storytelling, conversation, and laughter.

Our Native community was intertribal, with Santa Ynez Mission Band and Coastal Band Chumash, Tongva, and a few members of unrecognized California Indian tribes. It was also composed of many Native people from a variety of tribes originating from other states.

We gathered with an everybody-pitch-in-and-bring-something dinner. Roasted meats, fish, fresh from the sea to the plate. Platters of cracked corn, cornbread, hot from the oven with steam rising. Squash, fresh beans, salads, and bowls of tender greens. Wild rice. Green chili stew. Pumpkin soup, cooked from scratch in its own shell. Cookies made from acorn flour, ground by hand, the same way they did in the old days, along with rows of apple and pumpkin pies and chocolate cakes made by careful brown hands.

Initially, these gatherings began as a way to include Native students at the university who did not travel home to their families on reservations or in distant cities and were left alone on campus during the long Thanksgiving holiday weekend, since many Native American families do not celebrate Thanksgiving.

Our Harvest Dinner was born of love and kindness and is rooted in giving back to the community. We remember our strengths and make a strong statement that American Indian people are still here. Teaching our children Indigenous brilliance with a celebration of life: remembering our past, honoring the present, and doing what is necessary to walk a good path into the future.

Before we sit down to eat, we circle around. Sage is lighted. A prayer is said. Prayer for gathering knowledge, for strength, for survivance, for ourselves, and for future generations. Red-shawled women sing spirits home, calling for healing, giving thanks for the harvest.

The dancers begin, abalone shells swaying. I feel the heartbeat of the drum. Every year, for as long as I can remember, we have had the same host drum. All four drummers are our longtime friends. This year there are only three. One of our brothers has walked on.

We lined up for food. Elders first. After everyone piles as much food as their plate can hold, we sit down at round tables together. Now the laughter begins and the joking around. I am gathered with all of my friends. Memories circle and carry me back across decades of Harvest Dinners.

Frequently, I'm asked how I relate with the Chumash community and with California Indians, since as an Indigenous person, I am descended from tribes not of this locality. For me I have never questioned it. My sense of place comes easily and natural to me. I was born in California, in Tongva territory. Then, at age twenty-five, I moved to an area that makes up the traditional Chumash homeland. For forty-three years I walked gently, understanding I was a guest on this good Native land and responsible for holding the culture, traditions, and history of the Chumash people in my heart with deep respect. This California Native landscape has shaped me and has become a part of who I am. All my life I have lived on the border, with blood that is a mix of three tribes, merged, making me a woman who has become adept at respecting and honoring my place dwelling between boundaries.

All around me my longtime friends are exchanging news, sharing ideas, talking about Native authors, Native fashion, style, and art.

This dinner we share is also a time when we reflect on our traditions. Since we are a mix of many tribes, there is news shared and topics discussed reflecting a wide diversity of tribal identities.

At the end of the evening, when the drum plays a song for the elders and all of the elders get up out of their seats and go up to the front to be honored, as is our tradition, I notice my friend Michael is up there with them. It is the first time he is standing in the elder line.

I have known Michael from back in the days when we worked together within the American Indian Education Academy Project series "Tomol Trek." Michael is Chumash, and his wife is Eastern Band Cherokee. Their son and my son grew up together. Michael's son, an adult now, has become a paddler and has made crossings from the mainland to Limuw—Santa Cruz Island.

When it is time for everyone to get up out of their seats and go to the front of the room and shake the elders' hands, Michael says, "Get up here." He tugs on my arm, pulling me into the line.

"But I'm not an elder," I gasp.

Everyone all around me laughs.

"You're getting close," Ann says.

She raises her eyebrows, tilts her head, and regards me appraisingly.

53

WINTER OF DISTANCE

In early February 2020, Joy was again invited to the university, as the guest of honor at the Native student center. Now she was poet laureate of the United States.

The student lounge was filled that night. Looking around, I could see the faces of all my friends in the Native community, along with beautiful, articulate Native students chattering freely and bursting with Native pride. Their faces glowed. The coronavirus was not on our minds. It was out there, we were well aware, but it wasn't here, not in California, not yet.

A Native student, twenty years old perhaps, tall, alert, gently took my arm and led me to a seat in the front row, with the Native women elders. He motioned for me to sit down. As I slid into my seat, I saw the brightness in his eyes and the careful way he treated me with respect, as he would with his own grandmother.

Heat flooded my cheeks, but at the same time I felt peaceful, relaxed. The woman next to me smiled and patted my knee. Laugh lines danced around her eyes. My breath eased. Another elder took the seat next to me on the other side. One by one our row filled, and it seemed the most natural thing in the world that I should be sitting up front with the elders, instead of at the back of the room with the students or in the middle with the moms and dads with young children.

Once again, Joy played her music for us. She read to us. An hour-long conversation was launched, with the students asking Joy questions about writing. Sharing their concerns with their own writings, asking how she had dealt with writing dilemmas in her younger writer years.

I was relaxed in our shared Native essence, with the innuendos, the questions, the jokes, all not needing explaining. It was a good day to be alive.

At the end of the evening, a large crowd gathered around Joy. Many people lined up, waiting for a turn to speak with her.

Instead of joining in, I remained in my seat in the front row, watching. Listening. Deep listening, the way Marie, Mary Lou, and Wilma had taught me to listen.

Two weeks later, in late February 2020, the COVID-19 crisis began. It would be a long time before our community would gather socially again, with our breaths mingling in the air.

All my life I have heard it said that you can't be Indian alone. To be Indian requires community belonging, teamwork. In Indigenous communities there is an understanding that our lives play themselves out within a set of reciprocal relationships.

The virus raged, and our Native community held tight together, with prayer and ceremony outside, in the frosty air. Instead of shoulder to shoulder, we spread out and stood wide apart—ten feet, twelve feet, apart—with masks and other face coverings. Standing on the same mother earth, sharing the same sky.

Although we no longer walked the same sidewalks, we still brought food (and left it on the doorstep) when there was a death or a birth. When I burned sage alone, I filled my lungs with the breath of remembering, knowing our gatherings would return one day.

Meanwhile, I was returned to the river. All around me I felt the healing waters, as I became one with the river, finding my way as the river carved deep into new landscape.

When the shoreline of a river shifts from a storm, the waters surround the new form, and that shoreline becomes the new normal. During the COVID years, my life was like the river with the flowing movement of water. I knew that at some point the shoreline would return to the banks of its former self, but it would be changed. And while I could not yet see the contours of this new shoreline or the direction I was headed, I knew it had forever shifted the path from the one I was traversing.

I walked forward, changed for better, carrying wisdom from the strong Native women who believed I could and taught me how.

ACKNOWLEDGMENTS

This book is not only about me. It's also about the people whose lives are braided with mine, defining it and shaping me. To offer a measure of privacy, some names have been changed. What has not changed is the guidance they offered me, their love and the gift of their time they gave, helping me give to others.

I owe a debt of gratitude to many people. First, thank you, Heather Stauffer, my editor at the University of Nebraska Press. Your excellent editorial direction provided me with much needed guidance. Your insight and thoughtful questions let me know you could see where I wanted to go with this memoir but needed help to get there, and your suggestions for revision required me to write at a depth I'd not experienced before, for which I am grateful. Also, thank you, Elizabeth Gratch, copyeditor extraordinaire. Your expertise polished my prose, for which I am grateful.

Thank you, Margaret Randall, for saying the manuscript is compelling from the first word to the last and that it is an important story, beautifully told and extremely relevant for these difficult times. Your support gave me the faith I needed to go deeper to strengthen and improve.

With a handful of sentences, Denise Low turned me toward a steeper path, and I am forever thankful.

Robert Bensen, Allison Adelle Hedge Coke, Susan Devan Harness, Geary Hobson, Gloria Liggett, Diana Raab, and Kim Shuck—the support you have given continues to carry me.

I am a listener, and my family gave me a lifetime of storytelling. My friend Bill taught me how to get my stories onto the page. There are not thanks enough to Bill for teaching me to trust my memories.

Many thanks to Stacy Howlin Clark, a careful reader and early believer, and to Aurora Garcia, Maggie Thompson, and Liz Zok, early readers who kept me reaching.

Gratitude to everyone who reads Earth and the Great Sea Journal posts from my blog. There is no bigger contribution and inspiration to a writer's creativity than expecting her to sit down and write journal posts.

I am grateful for my family, for my beloved grandchildren, and for those who will follow us. May you always find support for your creative gifts, insights, and visions.

I thank my many teachers from the many directions, in all their many forms, who helped my journey begin and are helping to bring it home.

Help continues to arrive in unexpected ways. I would like to acknowledge my gratitude to the countless others who have helped with this book and to those helping in the future. While your name is not listed, you know who you are and of the role you have played. You are making my life and story rich, and I tenderly thank you.

Parts of this book first appeared in slightly different forms, and I would like to thank the editors:

Children of the Dragonfly: Native American Voices on Child Custody and Education, edited by Robert Bensen (Tucson: University of Arizona Press, 2001).

Fostering Families Today, May 2011, edited by Kim Phagan-Hansel.

News from Native California 32, no. 3 (Spring 2019), and 29, no. 2 (Winter 2015–16)

Santa Clara Review 108, no. 1.

Take a Stand: Art against Hate, A Raven Chronicles Anthology, edited by Anna Bálint, Phoebe Bosché, and Thomas Hubbard (Seattle: Raven Chronicles Press, 2020).

Unpapered: Writers Consider Native American Identity and Cultural Belonging, edited by Diane Glancy and Linda Rodriguez (Lincoln: University of Nebraska Press, 2023).

Unraveling the Spreading Cloth of Time: Indigenous Thoughts Concerning the Universe, edited by MariJo Moore and Trace A. DeMeyer (Candler NC: Renegade Planets Publishing, 2013).

Yellow Medicine Review: A Journal of Indigenous Literature, Art, and Thought, edited by Judy Wilson (Winter 2007).

We Who Walk the Seven Ways also contains excerpts from Terra Trevor's memoir, *Pushing Up the Sky* (2006).

Terra Trevor is a contributing author of:

Unpapered: Writers Consider Native American
Identity and Cultural Belonging (2023)

Tending the Fire: Native Voices and Portraits (2017)

The People Who Stayed: Southeastern Indian
Writing after Removal (2010)

Children of the Dragonfly: Native American Voices
on Child Custody and Education (2001)

CPSIA information can be obtained
at www.ICGtesting.com
Printed in the USA
LVHW031742140423
744393LV00003B/534